Understanding Gay Relatives and Friends

Understanding Gay Relatives and Friends

by Clinton R. Jones

A Crossroad Book
The Seabury Press/New York

1978
The Seabury Press
815 Second Avenue
New York, N.Y. 10017

Printed in the United States of America

Library of Congress Cataloging in Publication Data

Jones, Clinton R.   Understanding gay relatives and friends.
"A Crossroad book."
Bibliography: p.
1. Homosexuals—Family relationships. 2. Homosexuality. I. Title.
HQ76.25.J66   301.41'57   77-28704   ISBN 0-8164-2179-X

To Lucy Duff Grant
Distinguished nurse,
warm and gracious friend,
and to my other friends of
The Guild of St. Barnabas
for Nurses

Acknowledgments

There is no question that I must before all else express my appreciation to the Bishop, the Dean, and the chapter of Christ Church Cathedral, Hartford, for the total and unflinching support they have given me since the very beginning of my counseling ministry, and particularly as I have specialized in the area of human sexuality. It has been encouraging to me, and I would hope to others, that a particular Christian body has had the vision and the perseverance to consider such a ministry an integral part of its outreach and mission. ·

I would also express gratitude to the members of the Social Service Department of the Capitol Region Conference of Churches as well as the Board of Episcopal Social Service in the Diocese of Connecticut for their concerns in this counseling area and for the assistance they have provided.

In terms of the particular text I am indebted to my editor, William Gentz, of Seabury Press, who urged me to consider this project and who has greatly motivated me to complete it. I am grateful to Rachel Davies, also of Seabury Press, for her help and advice on many matters. My secretary, Helen Boynton, has been a never-failing support for more than a decade as part of my total ministry; in terms of this book I am particularly appreciative of her patience in typing my handwritten pages. I do credit my good friend Ann Angelo with ably preparing the manuscript for the publisher.

Many friends, some of them professional persons, have been

kind enough to read the early drafts of this text and provided helpful comments. Since some might be sensitive about their full names I will just say "thanks" to Kenneth, Jack, Nancy, Mike, Chris, Norman, Alan, Mike, Laurie, Bob, Jerry, John, Anne, George, Roy, and Jean.

Finally I do want to express gratitude to my warm friends, Bill and Betty Stremlau who so kindly provided me with the sanctuary of their delightful island home on Montserrat. It was inspiring to be able to write while sitting on a patio that looked out upon green, rugged mountains and the very blue Caribbean.

Contents

Introduction

"**W**ould you talk with my parents?" "May I ask my brother to telephone for an appointment?" "Now that I've told my wife I am gay, do you think it would help if you could counsel her too?" These are often the kind of questions counselees ask after they have begun to discuss their sexual orientation and their sexual feelings, which reflect preference for persons of their own sex.

In so many instances, perhaps the majority by far, family members and close friends may be the last persons to learn about an individual's homosexuality. This may not seem too strange. How true it is that people often share their most intimate selves with the person sitting next to them in an airplane or on a bus! There is a certain safety in such a situation since the chances are remote that a second meeting will ever take place. It may be an even more relaxed situation than traditional, formal, sacramental confession because there will usually be no censure, and surely no penance will be prescribed.

To confront family members or long-time friends with private, personal information that has usually been hidden and suppressed over a long period, many years perhaps, can not only provoke feelings of apprehension but can bring to the surface the fear of disapproval, even of traumatic rejection. Homosexual feelings, sexual encounters, even long-term interpersonal relationships, are not easily discussed in a society which has over the centuries been so negative, so judgmental, and so punitive concerning such matters.

Only over the last decade has the subject of homosexuality been surfacing significantly and there is now far more open discussion. Public forums, television panels, a plethora of new books and magazine articles, plus debates in legislatures, church councils, and professional societies, have now provided an atmosphere in which, at times at least, responsible, enlightened dialogue occurs. For a long time, the one place that a person could deal safely with well-guarded information about his sexual life was the clinician's office; but even here there could be some reluctance to deal with the tender subject of homosexuality. It is actually true that I have had many persons come for counseling with the final resolve to deal with their homosexuality, indicating that they had already been in therapy, often over a long period, but had not had the courage to admit to their true sexuality.

In a twelve-year counseling ministry which has had the specific focus of working with those who "because of sexual variation are in trouble with themselves, the law, or society" (an identifying phrase in the charter of the George W. Henry Foundation with which I have been associated), I have had the opportunity to relate on a one-to-one basis with more than two thousand persons. I have also organized several groups and have been their therapist, resource person, and/or advisor. Such groups include high school boys, a community homophile organization, transexuals, a Gay Alcoholics Anonymous unit, a group of married men who identify themselves as gay, a Church-affiliated gay organization, and various short-term groupings which establish themselves for some specific purpose.

None of us lives in a vacuum; we have whole series of interpersonal relationships. The majority of us have experienced the intimacy of a family; father, mother, brothers, and sisters. In some family constellations a growing child forms close associations with grandparents, aunts and uncles, and perhaps cousins. In the maturing years peer relationships are established; occasionally these last for many years, even a lifetime. There are the high school and college years where close bonds of friendship come into being. There are meaningful relationships with teachers, with youth leaders, with clergy. Then there are the particularly close ties between husband and wife, with children, and with the associations of employers and fellow workers. As already indicated, it is within some of these relationships that the homosexual person may feel the greatest apprehension about dealing with the most personal side of the inner self. Obviously, almost all persons are eager for acceptance. Understanding and appreciation is particularly sought from those who are the "nearest and dearest." For the homosexual person this does not always happen. Often, possibly too often, there is bewilderment, failure to accept, and even open hostility or outright rejection. It is for this reason that this book is being written. Considerable material now exists to help homosexual persons learn about themselves, to cope with some of their problems, and even to deal with the pressure and opposition they may have to face. What may now be needed is a text which is aimed primarily at what is often termed the "straight world" so that proper attitudes and responses can develop when the subject of homosexuality is faced in the family or between friends and associates.

During my counseling years I have had extended experiences working with parents, with other family members, with friends of counselees, with their associates—such as fellow workers and employers—and even with their teachers and their pastors. It is out of these relationships that I have gathered the material which will follow. Time and again, the first effort a homosexual person makes to "break the news" is to write a letter. There are times when breaking dramatic news by letter may seem wise. It provides time to think and reflect, and it may avoid some emotional outburst that could be difficult for both parties to handle. A response, if it is to be in letter form, can be more carefully considered and phrased. There may also be an opportunity to find objective help before responding. I would not imply that this is necessarily the best way of dealing with such a situation; I will say it is one way which some persons feel is right for them. Often counselees will bring such letters to me to ask my advice about them. There are occasions when I am requested to help prepare a letter. It has occurred to me that presenting letters of this nature might be a logical way of introducing each of the chapters of this book. Many of the letters which are included were written by counselees; a few have been composed on the basis of a particular counseling situation. Names and specific identifying references have been altered so that no one's privacy would be invaded. It is honest to indicate that what follows is not a result of theory but comes directly from the experiences of counseling.

1

Dennis–A Gay Son

Dear Mom,

Thank you for your letters. You have been a faithful writer and I have appreciated it. I haven't written for a while because I've come to some discoveries about myself and I wanted to be a little more sure of myself before I shared them with you.

Mom, I am homosexual. Now that I've said it, what is there to explain? In a way I wish we were talking about this face-to-face, because so much truth would be conveyed in a hug. But I think this letter will force me to express some of the feelings that have been unexpressed for so long. And I know you love me. I hope this letter will let you hear the words about me and feel my love at the same time, yet provide a breathing space so that you can absorb the information in your own way.

When did it start? I don't know. Although I am sure it has been there for years, I have uncovered it to myself only within the last year. I don't know the causes, either, but as I look back I see that I have been drawn to men—emotionally, psychologically, and in other ways—for a long time. It is an attraction that I had long considered a need for friendship but would admit to nothing more. At the same time, Mom, I was petrified of men. How strange all this is! I disliked appearing foolish in sports and I could never say the appropriately sexual things about women to other men. So I avoided those situations as much as I possibly could. Now, I am becoming more open to people in general, and especially to men, since that is where my great fear rested. After years of male scorn for whatever reason, I am meeting men who are accepting, open, responsive, and welcoming. I am more relaxed about life in general, and I find I laugh a lot more than I used to.

You know I respond very positively to women, and I always have. But I realize that I have usually wanted nothing more than human friendship from women (or girls, when I was younger). I rarely saw women as sexual beings. I realize that I just closed off the sexual part of myself altogether and tried to maintain some safe distance to fight against sexual involvement with a woman. Men always found it hard to understand my easy friendships with women. Now single women also find this "easy friendship" hard to understand.

Can you imagine how I felt not having (or allowing) the least inkling of these long-suppressed desires until only recently? It is a rather new world for me and there is a lot of exploring I have to do in it. I don't even know what homosexuality is, since it involves so much more than sex. I just find it comfortable to be with men sometimes (not all the time) in an open and free atmosphere. I am overcoming many of my own ignorant stereotypes about homosexuality. I do feel that I am learning a different set of behaviors and expectancies with people. Because I am more aware of my own sex, I see a lot more sex occurring between people in the most casual situations, for instance when a man "undresses" a woman with his eyes. I had been aware of these things in my head before, but not in reality.

Mom, we have never discussed homosexuality. I feel secure enough in your love to trust that you will see it as only a part of me. I need you now as much as I ever have, mostly because of who you are and who I am with you. With this revelation about myself, I need to know that you still see all of me—the whole person you have always warmed with your love and respect.

I love you,
Dennis

I s it ever fair to state that sons have better relationships with their mothers than with their fathers? Surely there is a great temptation to feel this, and there do seem to be many situations which bear it out. Without attempting any involved psychological evaluation, it is possible to draw the conclusion that if it can be taken for granted that the mother is a heterosexual person, she has certain built-in emotional responses which develop ties with her son that might not develop with her daughter. Then, of course, there have been many clinical situations in which it is quite clear that mothers can develop feelings of competition in terms of the daughter relationships. She may resent her husband's overexpressive affection for the daughter, she may be jealous if this daughter begins to exceed in areas where she is weaker, she may even know some inner anger when the maturing daughter begins to win the attention of interested males.

To some extent the mother is spared this competition with the son. Her own femaleness is complemented when she senses that her son cares for her, finds her attractive, is protective of her, and can even be openly affectionate. Again, this kind of response can provde its own difficulties. There are those instances in which the mother, if she should be widowed, divorced, or even single when the son is in his early years, showers the care and physical attention upon him that creates the kind of relationship that becomes too close-binding. This can also occur if the mother's relationship with the father is strained, and if he is not meeting her emotional needs. Her attempts to have these needs met by the son may result in a certain kind of emotional damage in the son which is all too difficult to repair.

It is a fact that in the past some therapists have wanted to conclude that this "close-binding, intimate relationship" with the mother can be a major causation for a son's homosexuality. I will presume that those who have had any long-term counseling experience with males who are homosexual will know of instances where such persons have established these deep ties with the mother and seem estranged from the father, but to use this theory to deal with the etiology of homosexuality is far too narrow because most therapists can enumerate a number of homosexual males who have poor relationships with their mothers and strong, good relationships with their fathers. A corollary is that one can find heterosexual males who, as sons, have unusually binding ties with the mother but who feel alienated, often severely, from the father.

In my opinion, although I cannot present any hard facts to back up the statement, I believe that if a son were on the threshold of discussing his homosexuality with a parent for the first time, he might opt to reach out to mother first. At least this is what Dennis, whose letter opens up this chapter, did.

What thoughts might be formulating themselves in the mind of the son who has come to the decision to share his long-kept secret with mother? First, perhaps, he may wonder what she already knows or suspects. There are situations in which the homosexual person may have thought others have little suspicion, if any, of his true self. Without his realizing it, family members and friends may be drawing conclusions from some various objective observations: he may now be in his mid-twenties and has not seriously dated girls; he seems to have developed some close friendships with other males; he does not indicate any intention to marry; he is secretive about what he does with his leisure time; he avoids those social situations which would require him to bring a date.

Taking for granted that he believes his mother does not know or suspect, certain priorities may be in his mind as he broaches the subject. He will surely want to establish the fact that he loves his mother; in return he will hope that no matter how shocking, how distressing, this news may be he will be able to keep and maintain his mother's love. Suspecting that his mother will have guilt feelings, he will try to the best of his ability to dispel what responses she may have in this direction. He may then want to assure her that he has searched his own mind in order to figure out why he has the sexual responses he has, but can reach no logical conclusion. He may even go on to indicate that he has already sought help through professional counseling with the hope that he might possibly change, or at least learn why he is the way he is. Possibly he will feel motivated to explain that even though he considers himself homosexual and is accepting the fact, he is not forsaking the value system which his family, his formal education, and his religious training have given him. Surely, according to the degree of the acceptance he has of himself, he will want to indicate that he is comfortable with his situation, relieved that he has come to terms with his sexuality, and at long last can relax enough so that he is finding a new inner peace and a joy which had seemed absent for a long time.

When there has been a strong, comfortable and a warm relationship existing between mother and son, then the son will have known considerable pain about having to withhold the information about his homosexuality from her. No doubt he will be able to think back to all the sharing they have experienced as he grew up. Even as a child, whenever he was hurt he could run first to her for sympathy and for help. When there were days of sickness and he was confined to room and bed, it was she who brought his meals, provided nursing care, expressed anxiety over his condition, and offered hope and encouragement about his recovery. As he had his interpersonal conflicts with other family members, with his schoolmates, or with his teachers, he could find her understanding ear. It was usually mother who waited up until he was safely home in the days he was beginning to drive the family car. There were the moments when, on coming home, his mother's door would be ajar and she would welcome his coming in to chat about the kind of evening he had spent. For a long time he had wanted to talk to her about how he felt inside in terms of his emotional, sexual feelings, but the courage could not be mustered nor did the right moment ever seem to occur. Deep within him there has been that expectation that if anybody will understand, she will; still, there also lingers that awful doubt that this information will strain her love too far and that he will finally be cut away from a support that has sustained him over the years.

When a mother receives a letter such as the one Dennis has written or has a personal confrontation with a son as he reveals openly for the first time what he conceives his true sexuality to be, then one can fantasize some of the thoughts which might pass through her mind as she faces such a realization.

It can be safely assumed that every mother would like her son to be "normal." Even from the moment of his birth she has these feelings. I recall one mother indicating that her immediate response upon the birth of her son was: "Are his ears close to his head?" In the very early days of a baby's life a mother is watching every reaction and response being made so that should there seem to be any abnormalities they could be detected early and obviously corrected as completely and as soon as possible.

Under the average situation she conceives her son as a male, wishes to see that he emerge with a gender identity which is masculine. As he begins to grow, his clothes, his toys, the way he is groomed reflect the masculine. She may even try to help him develop mannerisms and interests which are identified by society as being masculine. In the early years of school she will want him to follow the normal pattern of playing with the boys, learning sports, enjoying activities with the father, and being involved with youth organizations which place strong emphasis on activities, hobbies, and interests that seem typical for the average boy. At the secondary school level she will be eager to discover how he relates to the opposite sex: whether he is developing an interest in girls and how he is responding when girls begin to show interest in him. Then there may be the college years in which she will be anxious about what emotional attachments may be developing with members of the opposite sex.

It has been true over the centuries (although some distinct societal changes are now taking place) that it is expected the normal male will want to marry and raise a family. He will want to do so for several reasons: to accommodate his **sexual needs**, to prove himself a responsible person by taking on the obligations of family life, to propagate the species; and to establish a network of interpersonal relationships to dispel his loneliness, to give him a support system through the trials and tribulations of life; and finally, of course, to see that in his advanced years there are those who care for him.

These statements just made can be judged as idealistic, as too traditional, even to some extent as not usually attained; such may be true, but I would maintain they still represent the kind of expectation which a mother may have in her heart for her son's future well-being.

Few mothers who learn that a son is homosexual escape the feelings of guilt. She will usually say to herself, perhaps even openly to others: "Where did I go wrong?" The kind of questions that have been asked about the reasons for homosexuality over the years will be flooding her mind: Is it hereditary? She wonders if others in the past history of the family might have been homosexual. Is it a condition which could have been predisposed while the child was being carried? Did she care for herself properly? She might wonder if she had the right thoughts and attitudes. Could it be hormonal imbalance? Having heard the theories about the close-binding mother syndrome she may reexamine her relationship to the boy in his early years. Was she too affectionate, too over protective, too intimate with him? Did she do enough to foster a healthy relationship with the father and other males? Did she really help him adequately in the establishment of his masculinity? Did she try to keep him from involvement with girls? This list could be considerably expanded because there is this drive in the mother to find some way of taking the blame. This is common in mothers, especially in those who have children who are handicapped physically, mentally, or emotionally. Mothers whose sons in later life develop psychopathic or sociopathic personalities or become criminal react in the same manner.

What to say to this mother? Only one simple statement. At this point, regardless of all the study which has gone into the subject by psychologists, psychiatrists, sociologists, anthropologists, physicians, researchers, and scholars from all disciplines, there is no single answer that is definitive. The plain truth that the majority of responsible persons accede to is the fact that no one knows why human beings develop the sexual feelings and responses they have. There is some consensus that it is not through inheritance or some physical intervention before birth. There seems to be some evidence that sexual identity takes place in the very early years during what is termed the period of psychosexual development. For a mother to attempt to hold herself responsible for a child's homosexuality is not to be realistic in any sense of that word.

Other thoughts that a mother may have as she faces the reality of her son's homosexuality, grow out of her own feelings about herself as a woman, as a wife, as a helpmate. If she has, in her own concept of herself, been a good wife and has had a reasonably satisfactory or even unusually fulfilling relationship with her husband, she knows how important she has been to him in their years together. They have worked through a comfortable, satisfying sexual adjustment; she has stood by him through thick and thin; she has given him children and been faithful in meeting the requirements of motherhood; she has cared for his physical and social needs; she has been his hostess, made him proud through her contributions to the church and the community; and she may have been a direct help in his business or profession. In addition she may have brought financial assistance to the family coffers through a private income, inheritance, or her own working ability. All this would seem to give credence to our old phrase "Never underestimate the power of a woman," or another one, "Behind every great man there is a greater woman." These may be cliches, but there is perhaps much inherent truth in them.

In the final analysis, I believe it fair to say that the good mother senses her value as a good wife. Loving her son, she wants him to have a good wife. Now she has a new reality to face: her son says he is homosexual; he enjoys genital sex with men, not women; he has no intention of marrying and no desire to raise a family. It would seem as if he is opting to give up all the assets of having a wife and rearing children. Mothers want to be proud of their sons. When a mother talks little or seldom about her children, it is probably because she has literally consciously tried to control such a temptation. Few purses or wallets are without pictures of children. Who really wants to take away this privilege? Almost any mother has a built-in need to report her son's accomplishments, his successes, his happy adjustments to life. Mother lives in a "straight" society. No doubt most of her friends are straight. How many times has she dealt with the questions: "Has your son married yet?" "Is he dating anyone seriously?" "When do you think you'll be having grandchildren?" Mother may have harbored these same questions in her mind for a long time; now she has the answer: no serious dating, no marriage, no grandchildren. He is homosexual.

Mothers worry about a son's future. What will his being homosexual do to his career? What will happen if and when other people know? Suppose he actually "comes out of the closet"—all the way out! Might he not lose his job? Will he have difficulty living where he wants? Will he be ostracized from clubs, from business and professional organizations? Won't he be socially shunned in his church and in his neighborhood? Will his old friends desert him? What dangers lie ahead if he is involved in the homosexual sub culture?

Now, having thought about some of the feelings a son might have as he formulates his letter to his mother or contemplates that first open confrontation and, on the other hand, considering some possible reactions which might be generated in a mother's mind and heart, I would reflect on a specific point which is brought out in Dennis's letter. I would comment on his statement, "You know I respond very positively to women, and I always have." Surely there are many, many myths about homosexuality. Whole books have now been written to set out many of these and to dispel them. One of them, of course, is the fact that male homosexuals hate women. In the past there have been some psychiatrists who have pursued this line of reasoning and have even probed this concept with their clients. There have even been papers and theses built on the theme of male homosexuality as a flight from women. I presume there exists a clinical sampling which might support such a position. From my own counseling experience, however, I find little to support such a conclusion. The response I would make is quite to the contrary. I find that the majority of male homosexuals relate comfortably and congenially to the opposite sex. Not only do they respond adequately and happily to women in work situations, in social settings, and within the family structure, but they often establish close, rich relationships which may endure over long periods of time, perhaps for many, many years. They enjoy female companionship, appreciate conversation with women, often travel with them, even establish living relationships with them, and some are even comfortable in physical, affectionate, and sexual situations.

If the male homosexual can enjoy members of the opposite sex to the degree just indicated, how is he different from the male identified as heterosexual. Part of the answer rests in the word "preference." Given the opportunity of choice, he will want to respond to males rather than females. He may appreciate being in an all-male situation, especially if there is that common denominator of homosexuality. At such moments he can relax and be himself. No doubt, since he too has needs for close intimate relationships, he will be searching for persons with whom he can build a deep friendship; in fact he may be eager to find that "significant other" with whom he can establish lasting ties. It is, therefore, with a male, not a female, that he may want to make commitment and contract.

I do not want to leave out the important aspect of genital sex and all that is involved; anticipation, excitement, arousal, the act itself, and all the physical satisfactions which come through body contact. The male homosexual finds his greater pleasure in this regard with men, not with women. Many homosexual males may find pleasure in physical contact with women even to the point of genital intercourse, but here again we are in the area of preference—the preference is truly with males and the fullest satisfaction is in physical relationship to them.

Since this chapter is dealing with the mother-son relationship, is it possible to discover some positive comments about this situation? Mother's first reactions will no doubt be negative. She will think many of the thoughts already mentioned. It may take her some time to face the facts, to evaluate, to understand, and even to reach the point of acceptance. Can she move further? Is it possible for her to develop some positive responses? Her son, the one she has loved through the years, is still her son. She has hoped many things for his future. Is it unreasonable for her to continue to hope? She will not be helpful if her one and only hope is that he become heterosexual. To accept him as he is, this is what he asks. She wants him to know success in work or business or profession. Should she not continue to wish him the best in this area and help him in ways still available to her? She wants him to know love and be loved. Can he not find this in a person of his own sex? Although he may not know the joys and sorrows of the traditional nuclear family, are there not substitutions for this in a changing society so that he can experience satisfactions which will enhance his life?

There may be some other positives if she thinks about them. Father John McNeill, a Jesuit priest and author of *The Church and the Homosexual,* often discusses in his lectures the value of the single son or daughter in the family structure and how possibly this person has been the one "to maintain the home," especially as the parents reach their later years. It is his belief that often through the past this particular son might be the homosexual member of the family. Over and over again there are instances where it is the homosexual son who assumes responsibility for the mother when she is widowed. Since unmarried males may have had more opportunity to conserve their earnings, they may be in a more financially secure position to be helpful with parents who need care. I know of many situations where two homosexual males, having established a long relationship, "adopt" the mother of one or the other and provide many of the amenities and joys of life which she may well have missed in her earlier years. Through her son's commitment to another person she may not "have gained a daughter," but perhaps she can feel she has "gained another son."

A mother's love runs deep. She will not have lived without pain, disappointment, or anxieties, but she learns, too, how to surmount her problems, how to deal with reality, how to compromise and to handle change. So, her son is a homosexual! This revelation may be a challenge; may she find the strength, the insight, and above all, the love with which to resolve it.

2

Vickie–A Gay Daughter

Dear Dad,

I feel I must write this letter to explain why Jane and I have decided to move to Chicago. You know already that she has been offered a good job there which will be a real advancement for her. It would be foolish of her to refuse the offer. Although I do not have definite employment there at the moment, we have been given reasonable assurance that I will locate something rather quickly. No doubt you think I am not being wise in giving up my position here and moving into a city where I have few contacts.

You and mother know that Jane and I have now shared an apartment for nearly three years. We have traveled together, enjoyed common interests, socialized in the same circle of friends. I believe you have had a chance to know Jane quite well. I trust I am not wrong in sensing that you and mother have liked her; I know that she has grown fond of both of you and is appreciative of your care and concern for her.

For so many months I have wanted you to know that I love Jane; I firmly believe that she loves me too. This is why I must move with her. In her profession, opportunities to go forward with her career are few and far between; it is important for her to accept this new challenge. She will need help and support. She wants me to be with her.

I realize that all this may be something of a shock to you. Frankly, I do not know what you and mother have

been thinking about my relationship with Jane. You
have never asked any questions. We've had the feeling
you didn't want any answers. Now we agree we just
don't want to go on this way any longer. We want to
be honest.

You have been a wonderful father. I know you love
me. I know, too, you want the best for me. I suspect
you have imagined I would fall in love with a man, get
married, and have a family. No doubt you thought I
would marry Jack when I finished college. Yes, I did
love Jack in so many ways; I shall always be grateful for
what we shared, but I know myself too well. Our
marriage would have been a mistake.

I am happy with Jane; happier than at any time in
my life. Of course we have our upsets and difficulties,
but we do feel committed to each other. We are trying
to be realistic. Relationships such as ours know
pressures, particularly in a society which is often so
negative, but we are convinced that together we can
survive. We want our commitment to be lifelong. We
pray that it will be.

I don't expect you will want to answer this letter—
you never did like writing letters. Perhaps it needs no
answer. I, rather we, wish you and mother to know the
truth about us. We would like to avoid causing you
undue pain. Should you want to sit down and talk
about this before we leave next month, I'll gladly do
so; however, I think I'll let you make that decision.

Don't worry, Dad, I'm not being crazy; I'm sure I'm
not sick. I know who I am; above all I know I love Jane
and need to be with her. Please understand.

> *My very great love to you and mother,*
> *Vickie*

The *Father of the Bride* by Edward Streeter, a delightfully
humorous book which also was made into a movie in the
1940s, captured what many fathers go through when a daughter gets married. It was laughable when the father, weighed
down and frustrated with all the wedding preparations, drew

the young couple aside and offered them a substantial sum of money if they would just run off and elope. Although the father's nerves were in poor shape, I doubt whether he wanted to miss walking down that aisle with his daughter. That is a proud, high moment for any father. For him, it is emotion-packed!

The experience of the years would seem to indicate that daughters and fathers build bonds which have their very special character within the family structure. There is something particularly warm and touching as one watches a father in his affectionate play with his baby daughter. There is almost a special gleam in his eye. Even the sternest and most constricted male "softens" to the overtures of the little girl who reaches out to be affectionate. She evokes a response of tenderness, gentleness, and a desire to please.

Most fathers see their daughters in the traditional role. They enjoy seeing them dressed up, feminine looking, pretty. Now that we live in a world of unisex clothes (or identified more accurately, a world in which girls can dress in clothes once considered masculine), there must be a large number of frustrated fathers who prefer that girls look "like they used to." This does not mean that fathers are not managing to accept this change, nor does it indicate that the matter of dress is actually altering the feelings which are generated between father and daughter.

In the years before women began to find their fuller equality in the world of education, business, government, and the professions, fathers had one major thought tucked in the back of their minds: Will my daughter find a good husband who will support her and her children? I think of one father who had nine daughters; they all married. I have often wondered what kind of feelings were passing through his mind as he walked toward the altar with the last daughter.

The dowry is an intriguing institution. A formal one does not exist in America or in many parts of the world today. In ancient days it was important because inheritances were usually passed to sons but the dowry was one way in which daughters could receive some benefit from their family financial structure. In some countries the dowry was extremely important in attracting a bridegroom who might be considered substantial by the bride's family. To my knowledge it is still true in present-day Greece that the daughter of the family is given as large a dowry as possible, and often she, rather than the brothers, will be the inheritor of major family assets which are considered part of her dowry.

I make these remarks about the father's eagerness to see the daughter married and about the dowry idea merely to emphasize that society through history seems to place heavy responsibility upon the father with the expectation that he take seriously the problem of providing adequately for his daughter's future. Throughout the years her marriage has been the basic way her future could be secured.

Suddenly a father learns his daughter is a lesbian. How many of his fantasies dissolve? What kind of frustration is generated in him? How deep is his disappointment? Many apprehensions are apt to overtake him. How will she manage to build her security? If she marries a man, the law will give her protection because a husband must provide for his wife. Even if there should be a divorce, she has rights to child care, alimony, and to property settlements. At her husband's death, he cannot completely cut her out of his estate. On the other hand, what kind of legal help is hers if she enters a homosexual relationship? None! There can be no lawful marriage contract between two people of the same sex. It is true that persons can make wills; that wills can be changed and broken, that joint properties can be held, and this is some satisfaction. However, there is considerable evidence to indicate that court decisions have even upset joint agreements so that an individual may be denied what a deceased partner may have arranged. Although pension plans, social security, and certain annuities will protect a surviving wife, little assistance from these sources is available to the survivor of a homosexual relationship. If a father is apprehensive about his daughter's future as he weighs the value of legal heterosexual marriage over against the establishment of a homosexual relationship, he may very well be justified.

Does every woman want to be a mother? This is now a real question. History would seem to indicate that if she didn't want to be a mother, at least she ought to have this desire and intention. A reading of the Old Testament makes it rather clear that a woman's primary purpose was the bearing of children—many children. A man's future security was his children. His immortality, his name, the continuity of his family, must come to him through the children his wife would bear him. There is the argument that a woman is a "field to be sown." By nature, by God's will she is so constructed that it becomes her primary obligation "to produce."

Have times changed in this regard? Is this demand, this culturally imposed responsibility, still valid? Have women now come into a new position of dignity to the extent that they can be afforded the privilege of individual decision and choice. The social climate does seem to be shifting. The present emphasis on reducing the population, on birth control, on legalized abortion, and on bringing into the world only those children that can be provided a high standard of living is causing a major change of attitude. Most Christian denominations, for instance, no longer claim the primary purpose of sex to be the procreation of children; in fact, many clergy today are willing to solemnize marriages even when in premarital counseling they are informed that the couple has no intention of bearing children. There are instances in which sterilization and vasectomies are taking place before marriage.

What then can be said about the homosexual woman who is making it clear, because of her sexual orientation, that she intends an emotional, physical relationship with a person of her own sex. Obviously, there will be no child bearing. Can she be upbraided because she does not intend to marry, to bring a child or children into the world? Does this mean, however, that the homosexual woman has no mother instincts or is merely wanting to forego her responsibilities of bearing and rearing a child? Not necessarily. First of all there are many situations in which a woman, not knowing, or at least not facing up to, her true sexuality, has been legally married and borne children. At a later time, because of a variety of experiences, she becomes aware that she is not heterosexual but truly homosexual. She may establish a strong relationship with another woman, she (they) will want to fulfill the desire and duty of raising the child or children within the framework of this new relationship. Here, often, are the court battles. Lesbian mothers often lose because of society's homophobia. Usually there are mothers who have strong drives to keep their children, will go to many lengths to do so, but still may have to bear the pain of a negative judgment.

There has always been great debate over the subject of whether lesbians or male homosexuals, single persons or those in some stable relationship, should be allowed to adopt children. There have been instances where such adoptions have taken place. Adoptions, in my mind, always should occur with the greatest possible care and caution; but to place the single fact of a person's sexual orientation as the major stumbling block does not seem reasonable. Obviously there are heterosexual couples who have provided an inadequate emotional climate for children; in contrast, there are known homes established by homosexual couples which could be beneficial and provide many blessings for the maturing child.

One thought which has not yet been expressed in this chapter, nor in the previous one wherein consideration was given to the relationship of child and parent, is that the parent who has been particularly close to a son or daughter, and where a very real sensitivity exists, has a certain empathy in terms of the pain the son or daughter may have suffered in dealing with homosexual feelings. No person suddenly reaches a moment when there is the revelation that he or she is homosexual. There is a long, often tortuous trail stretching into the background. Dennis's letter states: "I have uncovered it to myself only in the last year." But then he goes on to explain how, as far back as he seems to remember, he was drawn to and attracted by persons of his own sex. In Vickie's letter she does not mention anything about her past feelings, just that she now is sure who she is and is convinced she is neither crazy nor sick.

Counselors who have had the opportunity to work at depth with homosexual persons will attest to the years of self-searching, of questioning, of denial which make up their histories. It is too difficult to know just when any child begins to sense that homosexual feelings, fantasies, and genital contact are not acceptable, that they may not be "right." Such a realization will vary from person to person. Suffice it to say there are those who will admit to early homosexual feelings with the indication that they felt guilty about them. Of course, considering the repressive attitudes about sex the Judeo-Christian western heritage has imposed, it may be that these negative sexual feelings were not necessarily because they were homosexual, but just that they were sexual. Boys who masturbated while conjuring up homosexual fantasies no doubt had guilt feelings, but the guilt may have been over the act of masturbating rather than because their thought patterns were homosexual.

Most enlightened parents today understand that in the development of the child there will be a period which psychologists identify as "normally homosexual." It is difficult to set these years too rigidly, but they seem to fall three or four years before puberty and shortly thereafter for males and a little later, possibly over a longer span, for girls. Some psychotherapists have believed that the man and woman beyond teen years who claims to be homosexual just did not successfully work through this stage of development and has merely gotten stuck in the middle of it. This is too easy a theory, if true at all; few counselors today will accept it. However, since we are discussing the pain homosexuals have known as they grow toward maturity, this is a time in life where they often know hurt. For instance: John is a homosexual male. He has always sensed and known this. At the time of puberty he knew he was attracted to boys. He liked boys' bodies. He liked playing the genital games in which they were all engaged. He was always scheming to get boys to sleep at his home overnight. He began to develop close emotional ties with certain of these friends. As the teen years dawned, he suddenly began to discover he was being rejected. When he tried to show physical affection to one of his friends he got the response: "Stop doing that!" When he tried to initiate genital play with those who were previously receptive he was told: "I don't want to play that way!" or "That's what queers do!" or "What are you, some kind of a faggot?" And so the rejection begins. Girls, too, have known this same kind of pain.

The high school or secondary school years can be particularly difficult for the homosexual. This is the period when the male is approaching the height of his sexual powers; the female, too, is sensing known sexual needs. Conformity, however, is the descriptive term for these years. There is little room for being different. To be known to be homosexual in these years is tantamount to social suicide. There have been too many instances of young high school people committing suicide because they felt they were queer and/or were severely ostracized by their peers. Often this is the period in which the homosexual person hides; this hiding creates pain and frustration.

The post-high school years, which may be spent in further education, the military, or the beginning of employment, can still be uncomfortable ones for the homosexual. Peer pressure can continue strong; the societal expectations to begin serious heterosexual dating are demanding; and the ambivalence one may experience about mixed sexual feelings creates many personal traumas. In my own counseling, I find that the largest number seeking help about their homosexuality are those between the ages of nineteen and twenty-five. During this period there are so many painful situations: relationships that begin and die too soon; fears about entering vocations in which revealed homosexuality could be disastrous; questions about providing the truth to parents and to other family members; anxiety over a developing promiscuous sexual life; guilt feelings and the sense of being rejected by religious institutions; the shake-up of what may have been a fairly secure value system; loneliness; shyness; fears of not being physically attractive, of growing old, of being arrested, of venereal disease, of being beaten up, of being robbed, of being blackmailed. Too often these days of youth have been termed happy and carefree. This may be true for some; for the homosexual who is trying to get himself or herself together these can be years of trial or even of terror.

Returning to Vickie's letter to her father, she may, as she confronts him with the fact of her homosexuality and with her determination to make a lifelong commitment to Jane, raise some deep-seated emotional responses in him which are directly connected to his own concepts of his manhood and his masculinity. Vickie has made it clear that she loves Jane and that this is reciprocated. In his own marriage relationship, considering that it has been a satisfying one and that he and his wife have known the pleasures and joys of the marriage bed, a father may very well believe that a woman to be fulfilled needs a man. How can a woman really meet the needs of another woman? When it comes to the sexual act she doesn't even have the right equipment! More than this, doesn't a woman really get turned on by muscles, a strong body, a hairy chest? In fact he may even harbor the thought that women are really most satisfied when a man is dominant, aggressive, takes control. How can this be between two women?

There is an aspect about lesbianism which can be threatening to men. Their masculine ego is challenged. There are many instances when men will deliberately go to bars where they know homosexual women gather. They begin to get upset when they discover that these women prefer dancing with each other and may refuse their invitations to do so. They may even try to make sexual overtures which when rejected begin to make them obnoxious. At times they get to the point where they grow aggressive enough to face up to some of the women and say "What's wrong that you'd rather have a woman than a red-blooded man?" They may even attempt physical force. A bar brawl may follow, with the arrival of the police soon thereafter. This may well be one good reason why lesbians have clubs, organizations, and bars which exclude men. They don't want or need this kind of confrontation and threat.

It is difficult for men to realize that women can make adequate love to each other and find in this lovemaking some of the satisfactions they might miss in heterosexual foreplay and intercourse. The truth of the phrase, "No one can make love to a woman like another woman" is difficult to prove, but it is a comment often heard. Therapists such as Masters and Johnson have been working to help in this area for several years. Their books and those of other clinicians have made the popular reading lists. From information provided by many lesbians, there is certainly solid evidence that their physical, genital, sexual life is more than adequate. As much as men may not like to believe or accept such a fact, there is little they can do to challenge the reality.

If Vickie's father does decide to answer her letter, what might be a reasonable response? Would he not do well to look on the positive side of the situation. Vickie is no child; she has finished college and is capable of working to earn her way. She has found a person she loves and who loves her. Their relationship has managed to survive three years, no doubt against odds. Jane is a woman he and his wife have had a chance to know and apparently to respect. The two young women seem to have a value system which meets their needs and, it would appear, which has not been too contrary to what he has taught her over the years. Jane has the security of a new position and the opportunity to move forward in her career. Perhaps it is good that Vickie can feel part of this and share in her continuing success.

Of course Vickie's father could react dramatically differently. He could be shocked, angry, condemning, even rejecting. He could cut off communication, break their relationship, threaten to disinherit her. With what result? Pain, unhappiness, fragmentation of a family, wounds which might never heal. Whether he will write or not is a question, but if he does, I would hope he might follow the gentle, understanding, loving way. This way he will make a daughter happy; this way he may very well know more peace in his own heart.

3

Bruce – A Gay Brother

Dear Betsy,

I am writing to discuss something with you that I have been meaning to speak to you about for the past several years, but I have not had the courage to broach the subject until today. You see, I'm gay. I know this is a startling revelation to you but try to sit back and think calmly about it for a moment.

Mama has known about my homosexuality for the past several years. She has not told you anything about it because I made her promise that she would keep it to herself. She has been wonderful about the whole situation; if it hadn't been for her support I don't know where I would be today.

Betsy, I am happy. I have discussed my sexuality with several professional people and they have assured me that I am not sick, I just have a different sexual preference. They have advised me to adjust to my sexuality and to live as happy a life as possible, rather than to attempt a futile fight against it.

You may be asking yourself: "But why is he telling me this now?" I am telling you, Betsy, because I am sick of living a lie. It is painful to sit with you and discuss a marriage that will never take place and children I will never have. This constant playacting I have been engaging in with you has been making me withdraw from you and the rest of the family because I can't cope with lying to those who should know the most about me.

I have kept silent until now because I was afraid this

news would damage our relationship. However I think in the long run that my withdrawal from you and the family would be even more destructive.

Betsy, I haven't changed. My "gayness" is nothing new for me, it is just a part of me that you and the family have been unaware of. I am still me!

Remember I love you. There is so much I want to say that just can't be written in this letter. Let's make a date to talk, I would be lying if I didn't admit that I am anxious about your reaction to all of this.

Love,
Bruce

T he depth of sibling relationships runs a full range. There are some brothers and sisters who seem to have established a closeness in their childhood days which manages to maintain itself all through life. The age difference is not an important factor. Often they may be close together in terms of years; on the other hand their birth dates may be widely separated, and in such instances an older sister may develop strong emotional feelings about a younger brother. It is never easy to learn exactly why some of these close ties are built. One might understand how a brother and sister could build long-lasting bonds if they are the only children in the family; however, it is not easy to understand how, within a family of several offspring two of them will seem to pair off and manage to keep in close contact throughout their years.

The mystery of human personality can never be truly fathomed. Why are brothers and sisters often so different? These persons have the same parents; they probably have had similar environments and have known like advantages and disadvantages, yet each one is a unique self. It may be important to realize, as many child psychologists point out, that every child born to the same parents has different parents than the previous child. Surely there can be considerable change in the emotional responses of a mother and father to the second child. The first one paved the way. The parents have now had the experience of a child; they have learned together how to establish their separate roles with this child; and above all, many of the anxieties and apprehensions about childbearing and child-rearing are reduced when the next birth occurs. Obviously there are many, many variables which make a family or a home environment different for each newly arrived family member: change of finances, family illnesses, vocational shifts, moves to another community, other family members who may be added such as grandparents, an aunt, an uncle, or perhaps the death of a close family member.

These general factors must be recognized in terms of brother-sister relationships, and they are set down here so that it can be understood why a person in dealing with a homosexual identity may pick and choose when the decision has been reached to make some revealing statement to a sister or brother. It is not too conceivable that he would want to start with the person with whom he has the least relationship, or with that family member whom he suspects will be more upset, less understanding, and possibly even condemnatory. In nature we learn that we deal with the path of least resistance; in our human dealings we are apt to follow the same course. When a stream is flowing and reaches a barrier, it changes its direction to seek out an easier way to reach whatever its destination may be. Families may function in somewhat the same way. The first reaching out is likely to be to those who will be loving and accepting; those who may be resistant and negative will be avoided as long as possible.

There are occasions when a brother may want to share with his sister the fact that he is homosexual, but if she is married, he may hesitate for two specific reasons: first because of her husband; secondly, he is not sure how the information will affect her attitude about his continuing relationship to her children.

What, then, about his brother-in-law? Here, again, the variables are far too many so that any kind of responsible statement is difficult to make. If the sister has seemed to establish a marriage in which the communication system is an open one, then this couple will be sharing their deep concerns one with another. Again, the brother who has normal sensitivities will not want, after unburdening himself to his sister, to ask her not to share this information with her husband. When she first receives such news, she may be considerably distressed. Many anxieties and apprehensions will overtake her. She may need to turn to someone with whom she can discuss the issues involved. It would be natural to reach out to her own husband. If she is asked to keep this secret from her husband, she will be setting up a certain block in their relationship. Should, for instance, the conversation with her brother bring about some change in attitude toward him, then, if her husband does not know the true facts, he will be questioning this change and continue to wonder what has brought about this shift in feelings. I am not sure I would want to set down hard and fast rules in this situation because it is in the realm of possibility that a sister's husband might be so rigid, so harsh, so condemnatory, so ignorant about homosexuality that attempting to cope with his negativism would be almost insurmountable. For her to keep her own counsel in this regard might prove the wiser course.

What will the sister who has growing children feel when her brother finally confides in her about his homosexuality? Unless she is particularly knowledgeable about the subject, she may grow apprehensive about his close contact with the children, particularly if there are boys. First of all she may have a reaction such as: "If my brother is gay, is there some chance this is hereditary and that my children may be affected?" This idea can be dispelled quite quickly since responsible professionals seem to be in agreement that a person's sexual identity is not a hereditary characteristic. However, a second worry may surface. "Will my brother try to be sexually involved with my sons?" With this thought she is caught up in one of the most prevalent of all myths about homosexuals: that they sexually molest children. Over the past few years considerable research has been spent on this subject. The overwhelming conclusion is that by far the majority of child molesters are heterosexual and not homosexual. A pamphlet published by SIECUS (Sex Information and Education Council of the United States) provides this kind of factual information. It is true that there are instances of sexual contacts between men and boys; but strangely enough the pederast is basically interested in being involved with children. Since he is usually heterosexual, he will prefer girls, but when such are not available, he will turn to boys with whom he may make easier contact. Little evidence exists to support the fact that male homosexuals want to be sexually involved with young children. The homosexual male is interested in males who are mature physically and emotionally just as the heterosexual male is interested in females who have reached full body development.

Possibly the most serious thought that will pass through the sister's mind, as she thinks about her brother and her children, is what kind of a role model he will provide. The fact that he is homosexual, that he accepts this, that he apparently will not be changing, and that even her children may be discovering this knowledge, makes her wonder what effect he may have upon their own emotional and sexual maturing? Perhaps the best answer to this question may be in how she may have regarded him up to the point of his revealing this new information to her. Has she previously been willing to have him in her home, around her children? Has she felt he has acted in any particular way which would make her embarrassed? Has he seemed to care for her children and related well to them? Is he genuinely and honestly fond of them? In turn, have they responded comfortably, happily to him? Has she been hesitant about leaving the children alone with him? Does he seem to have a value system acceptable and even admired by her? Has he been conscientious as a student? Does he work hard, and are his future goals being developed? Have her parents been proud of him as a son? Has he had a circle of friends who represent some of his own good qualities? If positive answers can be given to all or most of those questions, then why should this new information about his sexual orientation make any difference?

Intelligent people like to pride themselves on their lack of prejudice, but time and again those who consider themselves enlightened can suddenly feel blocked. There is the story of the son who, on returning home from college for the Christmas holidays, began to tell his family about the young woman with whom he felt he was in love. He began his description of how attractive she was, of her academic abilities, of her fine, accomplished family, of her church involvement, of her charm and popularity. Pleasure was being expressed on every side until he added quietly: "Oh, by the way, she is black." This same girl might have given her own family a similar accounting of him and created the same response with "Oh, by the way, he is white." There are many other words we could substitute for "black" or "white" and a whole set of negative responses can be registered in the hearer's mind. Blind prejudice is always a difficult challenge with which to cope. Too often, reason manages to make little headway when rigid and uncompromising attitudes stand so firm.

Throughout the years, society has wanted to establish the stereotypical homosexual person. Movies, plays, radio, and television, along with the jokes in the sophisticated cocktail lounge and in the "red neck" bar, have tried to establish a national image for those who are gay; but the scheme doesn't really work. Homosexual persons permeate the whole society; every profession and vocation, every Church and educational system, all social organizations and institutions. Occasionally one hears a person say "But I have never known a homosexual." There is only one honest response to this: "Indeed you have, but you didn't know it." By far the largest number of homosexuals are not "going public"; many are not even going to share such information with family members or closest friends. The so-called "closet" is bigger than all the world's mansions put together.

Various responses can be expected to the statements just made. There will be those, both straight and gay, who believe it is better if homosexuals stay quietly closeted. However, this can be countered with some particular points: First it is often the hidden gay person who falls into certain bizarre social behavior, is beset with guilt feelings, grows increasingly frustrated, and develops crippling emotional difficulties. Secondly, it is when persons "come out" that they find a kind of joy, freedom, and sense of worth which they did not know previously. Such is the story of Dr. Howard Brown who so ably tells about himself in his autobiography *Familiar Faces, Hidden Lives*. Thirdly, it needs to be stated that unless persons who have been already accepted, trusted, and honored by family, friends, and the wider circles of society are willing to identify themselves as being homosexual, the world will not be able to rid itself of the stereotypes which have been established by sheer ignorance in the past.

The pain of silence is known to the largest majority of homosexual persons. This fact comes through clearly in Bruce's letter to his sister: "I am telling you, Betsy, because I'm sick of living a lie." From the earliest homosexual feelings or experiences, a person may learn to keep silent. Of course it is the fear of negative reaction which causes this. This pain, often felt in early years, can go on and on. It can be presumed that some persons may live a whole lifetime without ever revealing their true self to anybody.

In contrast to the pain the homosexual person may know, one can sense the comfortable openness the heterosexual person is privileged to experience. As a teen-ager, a boy can brag to his chums about how well he "makes out" with the girls; girls, on the other hand can make it clear to their girl friends that they are attractive enough to receive plenty of attention from the boys. The young man can brag about his prowess as a lover; a young woman can talk about the number of men who seem eager to marry her. A wedding is a gala occasion; the honeymoon is an experience which family and friends hope will be a celebration of sexual joy and pleasure. Good marriages are thought to be those in which a couple are sexually compatible and in which husband and wife are meeting each other's needs. These days, as society is more accepting of sex being expressed in the later years, older individuals are proud that they are sexually active. Let it also be recognized that in the changing attitudes about sex occurring outside the bonds of marriage, people who are single, divorced, or widowed are not too hesitant about announcing that they are enjoying a sexual life.

Being able to admit to experiencing a sexual life is only part of the story. Heterosexual persons can be so open about their love feelings while, for the most part, this is denied the homosexual person. Very seldom can a man openly declare his love for another man; it is not easy for women to do so either. Many times such lovers literally have to deny the fact. There are few homosexual love affairs which are publicly acknowledged; no weddings, no announcements, no newspaper accounts, or pictures. It is true that from time to time gay couples will participate in the "blessing of a union" or "a service of friendship," but these usually take place in churches that have developed a special ministry to gay people. The services are quiet ones or they take place more or less within the limits of the gay community. When two men or two women who love each other establish a home, few house warmings take place; there are instances wherein they want to do it so quietly and unobtrusively that they hope few people will even notice that they are living together.

One of the greatest moments of pain homosexual persons know is when separation comes through death. Ordinarily, at the time of sorrow and bereavement, a person so stricken is surrounded by a well-established support system: there are flowers, messages of condolence, friends telephone and visit, food is provided, and various offers of help come forth. At the funeral home and at the funeral itself the person most bereaved is the focus of sympathy, love, and attention. This is seldom true when the bereaved lover is homosexual. There are instances when such a person hardly dares to let true feelings be shown or to be involved with burial arrangements because to do so would arouse suspicions on the part of others who may not have realized what the relationship truly was. Because homosexual coupling is without legal sanction, bereaved lovers often end up in situations where perhaps some distinct, basically uninvolved cousins make all the plans and decisions. The lover is made to feel like the "odd man out."

Love should be joyous, happy. Poets, song writers, and philosophers have been eager to make this clear over the centuries. When one falls in love there is the desire to climb the highest roof top and shout the news loud and clear. When two people reach that momentous decision to share their lives, they can't wait to tell the family, to notify friends, to let the world know. When the love survives the vicissitudes of life, its trials and traumas, its joys and satisfactions, then there is pride about the love. When death has brought the hard hour of separation and there must be the painful days of bereavement, some solace at least comes in being able to make it clear to any who will listen that a great love existed; there will be those who believe it will never die.

But for the homosexual persons, those who love, those who form relationships, those who may even maintain lifelong ties, there may have to be the pain of silence. Homosexual love has often been referred to as "the love that dare not speak its name." Can the homosexual be faulted for hoping for that day when, without censure, without condemnation, without rejection there can be the open, joyous personal proclamation that love has filled heart and mind and body? When will the world be ready to hear the good news?

Bruce is a young man in his early college years. He does not live at home nor in the community in which his immediate family lives. He is involved in homophile organizations and active in a Church that has an open ministry to gay persons. As he indicates, he has already been able to share his true feelings with his mother; she has been understanding and supportive. He has asked that she keep his confidence. He realizes that this has no doubt been difficult for her. Now he is eager to reach out to others in the family circle. It is time to test his sister and to hope that she can respond with the same kind of love shown by his mother. As this chapter has tried to point out, she may have her own set of reservations, but if she has some breadth of spirit, if she can discount some of the fears which in the final analysis have little foundation, and if she can know that he too wants and needs the kind of love she knows and experiences in her marriage and home, surely it can be hoped that when there is that opportunity to sit down and talk she can say: "Bruce I love you. I hope for your happiness."

4

Cindy – A Gay Sister

Dear Gladys,

I found the letter you left on my bureau yesterday. Since we do live in the same house, and you're not a deaf mute, I gather that you don't want to discuss your grievances face to face. Therefore my response will also be in letter form. Somehow I don't think you were expecting a reply since your feelings were stated like an official proclamation of holy admonitions. Well, I'm tired of being "baby sister." Just because you're older, don't think you have all the answers.

If I weren't so upset, I could simply ignore your letter and chalk it up to your way, not often very subtle, of putting people down. Frankly, I am growing tired of your self-righteous digs. Sometimes I think you act like Moses on Mount Sinai handing down the Ten Commandments. If you want to run somebody's life, why don't you get married and run your husband's? I don't really need you to run my life. So back off!!

I've already destroyed your letter. I felt that was best for all concerned. You can tear this one up after you read it if you wish.

Yes, if you insist on my putting it in black and white, I'm gay whether you or anybody else in the family likes it. All of your moralizing is in no way going to change the fact. Probably it would make life easier in this house if I were to lie and say that your suggestions about what I should feel and how I should act were helpful and I will therefore promise to go straight. But

I can't do that. I've always been gay and, although you may not be able to believe it, my being gay was not a matter of voluntary choice.

You say that you've tried not to lose all respect for me, but you have. Your ultimatum further states that in order for me to regain your respect I'll have to give up my association with "that woman." For your enlightenment, she does have a name. She is a person, not a condition! Barbara did not make me gay. I didn't "catch" my homosexuality from her as if it were some kind of a disease. We've loved each other for two years and, in spite of your bitchiness, that love has grown deeper and more meaningful to us both. No, I don't plan to give her up even though you think it may keep the family from some great scandal. If you think I'm living my life for the sole purpose of humiliating Mom and Dad, then you need to think again. They've never said anything to me; what they think is their problem. If they want to discuss all this with me, then let them do so. I hardly think they have appointed you as the family mouthpiece.

I know you are trying to make me feel guilty. As if I'm turning my back on, as you say, "what the family has stood for" over the years. Well, maybe I don't go to church as much as you do, but this doesn't mean I don't believe in God any more or don't know the difference between right and wrong. I guess, Sis, I would like to say, "Why don't you learn something about gay people?" Really they are not as bad as you seem to think. We're not all headed for hell in spite of what some of the Bible-pounding preachers scream.

I've reread this letter. It sounds as if I'm angry. Well, I guess I am, and I'm still going to put this letter on your bureau. However, I guess deep down you know I do care about us. I do want your love and I guess I want your approval, but I can't give up who I am. I can only hope you will try to understand and accept who this me is!

Cindy

"**W**hy don't gay people keep quiet?" "Why do a bunch of faggots need to parade?" "Don't homosexuals realize that if they'd stop being so aggressive, they might get the rights they want sooner?" These are the questions asked as a counter to the militancy which has emerged in the homophile movement. A minority, long silent, once intimidated and filled with fear, has found a new courage not only to be heard but to speak loudly—even to shout.

These questions might be expected from a majority whose value system is both challenged and threatened. Even those who consider themselves committed to justice, to liberty, to equality because of their religious tenets or their citizenship, are not always ready and willing to grant freedom to those whom they feel may, because of their so-called inferiority, have a right to be fully free. Was this not one of the arguments used in the black struggle? The majority believed the blacks were not ready, they were still inferior, they needed more education, they lacked an acceptable social sense. They even had a value system which didn't seem to match that of the majority. In the light of what has taken place, these points seem ridiculous, but I would claim that these were the kind of comments one heard as the civil rights movement was picking up steam.

The old phrase "Can there be evolution without revolution?" is always a disconcerting one. There is the temptation to want to believe that in a civilized, sophisticated society which is supposed to rest upon the Bible and the Constitution, violence is out of order. It could be argued that the French and Russian revolutions were successful because they had the basic support of the majority; however, it also may be fair to say that unless there had been the small bands of those who would risk the attacks, whatever they might be, the status quo might have continued. The great majority is apt to keep silent, to stay in the background, to risk little.

The homophile movement is in actuality a very young one. There was an amazingly hopeful period of emancipation which flowered in Germany at the end of the last century and in the early 1900s. Magnus Hirshfeld and the Institute of Sexual Sciences did a work of pioneering which deserves much praise; however, the advent of Hitler brought this advance to a sudden halt. Hirshfeld was discredited, the Institute and its large library destroyed, and in the end the homosexuals of Germany became marked (they wore a pink triangle) as were the Jews. It is believed that during this period about 250,000 were put to death.

After World War II there began to emerge in this country persons who bravely indicated they were willing to at least express compassion and understanding about those who were in personal difficulty because of their homosexuality. It was Dr. Alfred A. Gross who with others in New York City, chartered in 1947 the George W. Henry Foundation which has been a helping institution for three decades. In the early 50s there were the beginnings of the various homophile groups; some have come and gone, a few still survive and have significant contributions to make. In the beginning, those identified with such groups met secretly behind closed doors with the shades drawn.

The impetus for the gay movement as it is known today came out of what is familiarly called "the Stonewall Riot" which took place in Greenwich Village in June of 1969. Very briefly, this was a situation in which a gay bar was being raided by the police. In previous similar situations customers usually meekly did as they were told; this time, however, they fought back and the result was that the arresting police had to barricade themselves in the bar until they could be rescued. The riot went on for three days. In that short space of time "gay courage" was born, many "closet doors" burst open, and voices loud and clear began to be heard in all forms of the media. Gay marches, marking the Stonewall incident, now take place yearly in major American cities.

The above may seem an irrelevant or roundabout way to deal with Cindy's letter; in reality it is not. Cindy, young and gay, has been affected in one way or the other by the gay movement. It is not possible to presume from her letter that she is an activist, that she belongs to a gay group, or that she has ever marched in a parade; however, from the tone of her letter she makes it clear that she's not going to submissively accept the critical assault which her sister has apparently made upon her. Cindy is fully aware that gay people everywhere are beginning to stand up, to resist being pushed around, and to move on to say "gay is good."

Before reflecting further on Cindy and her feelings, it may be fair to try to discover what might have prompted her sister Gladys to write the first letter. It probably was not the result of some sudden decision; she no doubt had it in mind for a long time. She is older than Cindy. How much is not indicated, but a few years at least. Like most older sisters she probably developed some protective feelings toward her younger sister. As they grew up together, she was expected by the parents "to watch out for sister." She may have helped her learn to dress herself, guided her as she ventured to cross the street, kept an eye on her as she began her school years. If she were hurt, she might have administered first aid, been the sitter when the parents went out for an evening. She may have helped her learn to swim, and assisted with some of her school projects. For one period they may have shared the same bedroom. Their lives may have known separation during the college years, yet they probably shared holidays and vacations which brought happy times.

Being older, Gladys may well have been admonished by the family to serve as a good model for this younger sister. No doubt having to set an example was burdensome time and time again; however, she could have felt this to be her duty. She may even have wanted to do this. She did have her specific standards which were meaningful and satisfying to her; obviously she would want her sister to share, to accept this same value system. Apparently Gladys was conscientious about family responsibilities—she lived at home and probably assumed a useful role within it. She may be employed and assisting with family finances. Being heterosexual, she may have been looking forward to marriage but such an opportunity had not yet come.

Gladys felt that the Church was important. It would seem that she took church attendance seriously and may well have been involved in various activities. It may be that she was teaching on Sunday mornings. From this background, she is obviously taking the position that homosexuals are sinful.

The knowledge Gladys has about homosexuality seems narrow and limited. She seems to have the idea that being homosexual is a matter of individual will and of choice. Since she is straight and her sister shares the same parents and the same home, has known the same advantages of education and social environment, how could her sister be so different? The only logical conclusion which seems possible in Gladys's mind is that Cindy is being perverse. Possibly out of rebellion or just wanting to be different, she is consciously opting to be gay.

Cindy's relationship to Barbara apparently grew more and more threatening to Gladys. Barbara is older. Without realizing it, Gladys may have developed some feelings of displacement. In times past, Cindy probably came to her for help and advice; now she seeks out Barbara. There were times when the two sisters went to a movie together or went shopping; now Cindy does these things with Barbara. Being a close-knit family, the members enjoyed many common events: picnics, Sunday dinners, birthdays, holidays, and church affairs. Cindy skips some of these now so that she can be with Barbara.

There is an overtone in Cindy's letter which seems to indicate that her sister believes that Barbara has "made" her gay. If Gladys has such a thought, she may only be reflecting what so many people still are convinced is true. One of the great myths about homosexuality is that it is taught. So often homosexual persons are attacked on the basis that they are eager to increase their ranks by a certain "missionary effort." Some extreme critics have even gone so far as to claim that "since homosexuals don't produce, they must seduce." I have to consider this as one of the most ridiculous statements ever made. I do so on the basis of two simple points: first, seduction does not make persons homosexual; and secondly, I am fully convinced that the majority of homosexuals, recognizing the negative attitudes of society today about homosexuality, would not wish such an identity upon anyone else. Most homosexuals have known far too much pain in their lives to want to proselytize.

Obviously, Gladys is convinced that homosexuality is sinful. To attempt to discuss such a point throws us into an arena in which one side shouts "It is!" and the other screams back "It isn't!" One is reminded of two small boys arguing about the best car. "Ford's best—my father says so!" the other replies "Chevy's best—my father says so!" It is a difficult spot for an arbitrator. The battle lines in this confrontation are not over being homosexual. Even the most conservative and traditional religionists will not condemn a person because of homosexual orientation, the issue centers on physical, genital acts between persons of the same sex. It is understandable why certain moralists and theologians have felt that such acts are sinful, because throughout the centuries the Judeo-Christian sexual ethic has been a narrow one. Plainly spelled out it has said that no person, male or female, may engage in a sexual act with any other person until marriage, and then these persons are in an exclusive sexual contract until the marriage ends, which in the eyes of some Christians can come only through death.

In my mind, the serious dilemma is this: if religious, societal permission is given persons of the same sex to engage in genital acts, then this will negate the ethic which has been long established and therefore a new sexual freedom must be granted all persons. This, many argue, will undermine the basic foundation of marriage and the family, with the result that our whole social structure will be weakened. There are those who do make the suggestion that homosexual persons have not chosen their sexuality and should not be denied expression of genital sex, but at least let them take on the same responsibilities which heterosexuals assume through a marriage contract. This makes interesting theory, but up to this point no state in this union, and no western country to my knowledge, is willing to grant a marriage license to two persons of the same sex.

How can this knotty issue be resolved? I doubt that theologians will be the effective instruments. I am of the opinion that the homophile movement, like the civil rights movement and the women's liberation movement, will not be deterred. Acceptance will come little by little. Adversaries will win a battle here and there, but forces which lie behind sexual freedom will win the war. I do believe that David Mace may be right when, as far back as 1970, he said in his book, *The Christian Response to the Sexual Revolution,* that the "sexual revolution is already over; all we have to do now is catch up to it." Sexual change is all around us; we will not escape it.

We do not know the particular Christian denomination to which Cindy's family belongs. This may not be important, but at least Gladys may truly believe that if a person has enough conviction, enough spiritual depth and has faith in the power of prayer, dramatic changes can take place. Those who know the Bible are familiar with Jesus' healing miracles—healing of the sick both in mind and body; he even had the power to raise the dead. Others of faith also healed both in Old Testament days as well as in the body of fellowship called the Church, whose members had been infused by the power of the Holy Spirit.

This healing ministry still continues. There are particular individuals who are identified as possessing the power to heal. Even within many of the articulate, sophisticated main-line denominations, there are healing missions—the "laying on of hands," retreats and conferences on the subject, and persons both clerical and lay who are recognized as having the special gift to heal. Then, too, there are the more popular healers, some of national fame, who even have healing programs on radio and television. What is always expected in the healing experience is the faith of the person who is sick. Even Jesus said this often: "Thy faith hath made thee whole." The desire to want to be healed and an absolute faith that God does heal —this is the important combination.

How does all this apply to persons who are homosexual? First of all, is the homosexual sick merely because of his or her homosexual orientation? There is not full agreement here. Through years past, such has been the belief. In ancient days there were times when it was thought homosexuals were possessed with an evil spirit. With the rise of modern psychiatry, the decision was that the homosexual was diseased. Salvation could only come through long, extended therapy. Now, since 1973, through the action of the American Psychiatric Association, homosexuality has been removed from the category of illness. As Dr. Howard Brown facetiously remarks in his book, *Familiar Faces, Hidden Lives,* "Never in history had so many people been cured in so little time." This was not a unanimous opinion, and there are psychiatrists and therapists who honestly believe that homosexuals are sick and need treatment.

The gay world stands solidly opposed to the sickness theory. Admission is made to the fact that some homosexuals have emotional problems, some are deeply neurotic, a few are psychotic; but such can be said of the heterosexual world, too. Homophile leaders try to point out that the reason some homosexuals have difficulties is because the straight world is cruel, oppressive, and unreasonable about homosexuality. It pressures gay people to conform, to deny themselves, to adopt a life-style which is misfitting so that there is frustration, failure, and anger which result in personality distortion.

The gay movement has reached enough strength so that counter movements begin to rise. One of these is based on the premise that homosexuals who express their sexuality in any genital way are disobeying God's word as it is to be literally interpreted in the Holy Bible. Homosexuals who do not make every effort to change their ways, to give up their sick, sinful behavior are being disobedient in their refusal to let God's will and power take over their lives. Some determined advocates of this position are very critical of therapists, counselors, educators, doctors, clergy, and, of course, gay movement leaders who take the position that homosexual persons should learn to accept themselves and make every effort to live their lives without attempting or hoping for a change in their sexual orientation.

Certain of these biblical literalists are convinced that if homosexuals will pray, if those who are trying to help them will also pray, then the right change will begin to take place. Anyone who believes in the Christian faith will no doubt be ready to say with Holy Scripture: "with God all things are possible." But there are also those who may be justified in believing that the psychologists, the social scientists, the biblical scholars, and the theologians who bring new light and knowledge about homosexuality may also be instruments of his truth.

From a counseling point of view, I am tempted to make a comment about those who feel that right praying will be effective. Over the years there have been very few counselees who, when they reveal their homosexuality, do not explain that they prayed, read the Bible, went to confession (over and over again perhaps), did penance, attended Mass, made their communions, been on spiritual retreats, sought out clergy for counseling, often been through long, arduous spiritual disciplines, yet their homosexual feelings didn't disappear. Such persons are struggling through many guilt feelings. When they are told that some homosexuals have been "cured" by God's power, then their sense of guilt is doubly increased. It is natural for them to respond with, "If God healed them while I have prayed and prayed and prayed without being changed, then I must be really bad. God must especially hate me." I find that homosexual persons usually have all the guilt feelings they need; I, as counselor, hardly should try to increase them.

Before I leave the subject of the biblical literalists, I do think it has to be said that they represent one point of view. The other side of the picture comes out of the work of biblical scholars who are presenting new interpretations of some of the traditional biblical texts which are understood to be condemnatory of homosexuality as we understand the subject today. A pioneer work was done by D. S. Bailey, *Homosexuality and the Western Christian Tradition,* and as already mentioned, the more recent work, *The Church and the Homosexual* by John McNeill, S. J.

Gay leaders, especially people like those who make up the Board of the National Gay Task Force (80 Fifth Avenue, New York City) are stressing that being gay is no block to good health, to success, or to happiness. Through their publicity, their radio and television programs and their political and educational channels, they tell the story of prominent men and women—doctors, lawyers, psychiatrists and other counselors, clergy, senators, prominent businessmen, educators (the list could go on and on) who live full, productive lives but who are openly gay.

The exchange of letters between Gladys and Cindy set forth the opposing positions with which society as a whole is being forced to deal. Gladys thinks her sister is sick—if not sick, then at least willful, stubborn, recalcitrant—because she seems to be making no effort to change. Cindy, on the other hand, is fighting back. She says she is the way she is through no fault of her own. She did not try to be homosexual. She does not know how she got this way and since no one else knows for sure, then she is of the opinion that neither she nor anyone else is going to make her straight. She makes it clear that she didn't "catch" her homosexuality from anyone else. She feels she is privileged in having found someone to love who seems to love her—theirs is a good relationship in her eyes. She has apparently worked hard and successfully for her education. She doesn't seem unhappy about life. She has not lost faith or a value system; she believes in God. All she wants is for Gladys, for the other members of the family—yes, everybody else perhaps—to "get off her back" and let her live her life.

5

Arthur–A Gay Husband

Dear Millie,

I presume you will think it strange that I am writing
this letter to you. After our many years of marriage
and all we have shared together, a letter may seem
artificial. On the other hand, there are moments when
having to sit down and actually put a few thoughts on
paper can make things clearer and more concise. Often
when we talk together we get so emotional that we
don't end up saying what we want to say. I can't speak
for you, but after such experiences I think to myself
"But why didn't I say this or that?" or "If I'd had
more time to think I would have said it differently."
This is why I thought a letter might help.

Obviously I want to deal with the subject which has
upset both of us and our marriage for the last several
months—my homosexuality. It is still difficult to believe
that my revelation of it was such a shock to you and
that you had no suspicions. (I had no idea I was hiding
it so well!) I have been grateful that at least you have
appreciated the pain I have known all these years. I'm
sure there are wives who would be totally
unsympathetic.

I trust you are glad that we've both sought
counseling, individually and together. This has not
been easy for you, I know, but I feel we must admit
that it has been helpful to reach out to someone
objective and knowledgeable. At least it has made both
of us conclude that I'm not dealing with some passing

fancy nor that I'm on the edge of an emotional breakdown.

Do believe that I am trying to be a sensible, responsible person. I am not taking our marriage lightly, I never have. Now that Nancy is in high school, I want to try and be the father she needs in these years; but frankly, I'm not sure just what this means. No doubt you agree with me that this is not the time to tell her about myself. That, of course, may have to come.

I am still too mixed up to know where our marriage is going. You already realize what you have meant to me through the years. It is still good that we can be close together at times. I have to be honest when I say I can't be sure what the future holds. My homosexual feelings don't go away or diminish. You've known about that fleeting affair with Ernie, but this is over. What worries me is what will happen if I get involved again.

All I guess I want to say right now, Millie, is that our marriage is important to me and I love you and Nancy. I'm going to stay in counseling and, although I may not have the right to ask you to do so, I hope you'll be able to stand by until together we can see what the future holds. Finally, I guess what I'm trying to say is: "Thanks, Millie, for being you!"

Arthur

P. S. Perhaps it will be wise if you destroy this after you read it.

C an marriage be a way to escape one's homosexuality? Many have thought so. Has the plan worked? How could any solid statistics be compiled? The one fact that can be truly stated is that there are surely instances when this hope has not been realized. Counselors who try to help those who are struggling with their sexual identities, their anxieties, and their relationships are in a position to comment at some length on a growing number of men and women who have married but eventually come to a point in their lives when they need help in their effort to cope with their homosexual feelings.

In the very beginning of my own counseling, I remember a distinguished man of about sixty opening our first session with "Can you help me get a divorce?" His was a story of getting married when he was nearly forty. He had always known himself to be homosexual. He had fought this all his life. Finally he felt that if he married a woman who seemed deeply in love with him, he would be free of these painful homosexual drives. He and his bride seemed to have many things in common intellectually, culturally, socially. He admired her and had grown fond of her. His bachelorhood was not very satisfying. He wanted a home, a person with whom he could share; he was eager for societal approbation. The marriage began well, but he realized as the years passed that it had been a mistake. They began to drift further and further apart. They had even reached the state where they had established their own friends, developed interests they did not share, and even taken separate vacations. He made it clear that he wanted a few years of freedom. He didn't expect to undertake a blatantly open, gay life-style, but he did want to feel liberated enough to enjoy experiences and persons he had been denied. He did file for his divorce, but before it could be final, a fatal illness brought about his death. As I read the obituary which spelled out his successful career, I wondered if anyone else knew some of the inner pain this man had known and how he had yearned for some emotional fulfillment that he felt he had denied himself.

Ours is a world of surveys, statistics, and computers. There is always that drive and demand to know: How many? How often? The physical sciences are always measuring, the social sciences keep presenting new data, and the psychological world continues its struggle to establish its own defined norms. The matter of human sexuality has not been neglected. The Sex Institute at the University of Indiana in the 1940s made a serious attempt to deal with the subject of human sexual response. The published books: *Sexual Behavior in the Human Male*, 1948, and *Sexual Behavior in the Human Female*,

1953, are filled with graphs and percentages. These results have been applauded by many over the last two or three decades, while at the same time there have been the challenging critics. However, these particular statistics remain the most widely quoted, especially when the subject of homosexual response is being discussed.

Using the so-called sex-rating scale the researchers concluded that four percent of the male population and two percent of the female population of the United States is primarily and predominantly homosexual in terms of sexual response. With a present population of two hundred million this would suggest that about twelve million men and women in this country are basically or exclusively homosexual. Another statistic indicates that thirty-seven percent of the males studied and twenty-eight percent of the females interviewed admitted to a homosexual genital experience to the point of orgasm at least once in their lives. Since this survey could not deal adequately with the question of latent homosexuality, one does have to conclude that no doubt there are more persons who have homosexual feelings, but who may not act them out, than had been previously believed before the completion of this particular study. Further statistics from the Kinsey study indicate that 18 percent of American males are as much homosexually orientated as heterosexually between the ages of 16 and 55. Therefore on the basis of our present population there are about 16 million males who fall in this category.

The sex-rating scale is divided into seven points. A person is put at the zero end of the spectrum if the identity can be considered totally heterosexual, meaning that from an emotional, sensual, and genital point of view the sexual orientation is toward those of the opposite sex. The other end of the scale, six, is for those whose total sexual outlet is homosexual. It now seems as if the majority of persons fall somewhere between these two extremes. Surely persons who are exclusively homosexual all through their lives are rare; likewise, the number of exclusively heterosexual persons is far less than was once suspected.

Today the subject of bisexuality or ambisexuality is being discussed at some length by students and researchers within many professional disciplines. Along with these serious evaluations, there are popular magazine articles, books, plays, and movies which deal with this theme. It is a temptation to believe that true bisexual persons will be a number three on the sex rating scale, equidistant from both the homosexual and the heterosexual extremes. In my opinion, such is not the case. I personally do not believe that there is an individual who is a true "three." Experience seems to indicate although the incidence of bisexuality is high, those who register such feelings fall on either one side of the scale or the other. I still maintain that the determining word is "preference." Over and over again, as I have attempted to help counselees to an understanding of their sexuality, the issue of preference has surfaced. Up until the present I have not had a person say "It doesn't make any difference whether I am sexually involved with someone of my own or of the opposite sex." Such a person may frankly indicate they can or they do act out sexually with both sexes; but when asked to make a choice, they will say "I'd rather be with a woman," or "I'd prefer a man."

There is the temptation to presume that it is the person on the predominantly heterosexual side of the scale, but who may also have a homosexual component, who enters into marriage. But this cannot be taken for granted. Many times men and women who can be determined as being basically, predominantly homosexual will marry. The question which therefore arises is: "Can these marriages survive?" There is no hard and fast rule. The variables are too many. Two counseling situations may provide some explanation:

Jim has been married for sixteen years. He has three daughters. Deep inside he always knew he was homosexual. There had been many homosexual encounters and affairs in his earlier years. In graduate school he met his wife—charming, attractive, intelligent. They shared much in common. They fell in love and were married. Professionally he also felt that marriage was best for him. The sexual relationship with his wife was always poor. It grew less and less frequent. His wife did not seem frustrated by the eventual decision to cease their sexual encounter completely. Even shortly after the marriage, he began his clandestine homosexual "acting out." This was continued. Although he has established comfortable friendships with other homosexual males, he has no desire to enter into any close, intimate relationship nor to make specific commitments which might threaten his home or marriage. His wife is cognizant of his homosexuality and, although not overjoyed about it, remains tolerant and understanding. Neither has any intention of ending the marriage. The home is a basically congenial one; apparently the children are not cognizant of their father's homosexuality.

Sam's situation is different. He married shortly after he came out of the service. Within two years their son was born. He had not mentioned his homosexual orientation to his wife prior to marriage; in fact, since he felt adequately satisfied sexually in a heterosexual situation, he did not feel that the desires he felt for men would bother him. This was not totally true and when he finally did get involved homosexually, his wife, through a set of unusual circumstances, learned of his infidelity. When he was challenged by her, he admitted his guilt and then tried to make it clear that although he had these homosexual tendencies, he did love her and their son, wanted to keep the home, and would seek counseling to try to cope with his problems. In this instance, the wife could not or would not visualize a life in which she had a husband who was going to have to struggle with this kind of temptation or frustration. She felt there was no other way out of the difficulty but to file for divorce, which she promptly did.

From a counseling point of view I would identify Jim as primarily homosexual; Sam as basically heterosexual. Both can be said to be bisexual. As indicated, Jim's marriage survives while Sam's is ending. What is the variable? In the case of these two couples, the attitudes expressed by the wives made the difference: one was willing to live with the reality of her husband's homosexuality; the other would not try to cope.

There is enough clinical evidence to show that the opposite of the above can be true. There are many situations in which men who are primarily homosexual marry, perhaps in the late teens or early twenties when sexual drives are especially strong. They will do so with good intention; often they will hope that having a wife will soon dispel their homosexual feelings. Sometimes it is not too long before they know their error. They begin making sexual contact with men, they grow less and less interested in their wives—they may even become impotent with them. Wives begin to feel inadequate; there is frustration on all sides and eventually the marriage breaks. On the other side of the scale is the man who is primarily heterosexual. He is happily married, with home and children. He does, however, have a homosexual component within him. At times, under certain emotional pressures he may get involved with another man. These are usually cursory and infrequent experiences. He probably will not feel he wants his wife to know. He doesn't seem to feel such episodes are any threat to his marriage.

Again, men who fall into such categories have to be termed bisexual. In these situations, in contrast to the accounts of Jim and Sam, it's the predominantly homosexual male who can't carry through with the marriage while the primarily heterosexual husband can do so while still incorporating some homosexual activity which doesn't emerge as a serious problem to him.

The increasing number of married men who have come to me for counseling brought me to the decision to organize those interested into a group which has now met regularly for many months. It does seem that it has been important for them to have this opportunity to share together and to actually establish a kind of fellowship amongst themselves. The majority have been persons in various professions. They have had much in common; there seems to be a consensus that through these sessions they have been helping each other. It was not long after the group established itself that there were two obvious divisions almost equal in number. There were those who have every intention of staying within the marriage relationship; in some such instances they are in joint counseling with their spouses. On the other hand, several were in situations in which, either through their own choosing or because of the wife's decision, separation or even divorce would no doubt be inevitable. At times these two subgroups have met separately in order to deal with the particular dynamics of their own marriage status.

One of the variables not yet discussed concerns the homosexual husband who eventually falls in love with another man and this relationship grows deeper and more intense. Little by little he realizes that he cannot be truly happy and satisfied until they can make a binding commitment to each other which may even mean establishing their own home. How soon this happens may also depend on the lover's feelings. I know few homosexual males who are eager to be "home breakers." In fact it is quite true that some homosexual men will not even consider "dating" a married man; for them the inherent problems are just too many and too great. There are others who may be willing to be involved with men who are married, providing their relationship doesn't appear to be growing too serious, simply because they do not want to find themselves in the awkward position of "the triangle" with all its built-in traumas. It must be stated, however, that controlling the strong emotions which are identified with human love may not be easy. Men drawn to each other may suddenly come to realize that they have developed an interdependency, a need to be with each other, and have found deep satisfactions which they would find too devastating to end. The wife involved may be understanding, may be willing to make concessions, may be eager to keep her marriage even at the high price of sacrificing her own needs, but even this kind of cooperation or sacrifice may not be adequate, and the break comes. The complications and mixed emotions which mark entanglements such as these result in travail and pain for all concerned.

It is after reading a letter such as Arthur's and on sensing some of the hurt and unhappiness that comes to married men who are homosexual and to their wives as well, that one is tempted to raise the question: "Would it not be better if homosexual men never married?" An easy answer would be "Yes, of course." But it isn't possible to subscribe to such a conclusion. Several reasons can be cited:

First, there are instances in which persons have not really known or at least accepted their homosexuality until after marriage. Latent homosexuality is a reality. Maturing males will deny, fight back, sublimate their homosexual feelings for years. At the time of marriage they may never have experienced an overt homosexual encounter. Also, they may not have had many or any genital experiences with the opposite sex before marriage. It is possible that having begun to act out their sexual responses and needs heterosexually, their hidden homosexual feelings begin to emerge and these may end up being their dominant feelings.

Secondly, homosexual males, as perhaps has been already adequately stated, may hope that a good marriage, a loving wife, will be a way they can "beat the rap" and through the experience of the marriage bed, the homosexual feelings will just fade away. Clinical evidence does not seem to support this expectation.

Thirdly, many men who are homosexual, have strong paternal drives and feel they need and want children; therefore marriage seems the only course. This subject will be discussed more fully in a later chapter.

Fourthly, a homosexual man may marry for the sake of his family. This is particularly true of those with certain ethnic or religious backgrounds. The expectation that he produce children, that he take his rightful place in society, and that he see that the family name be continued is a responsibility which is difficult for him to abrogate.

Fifthly, men who marry and who are already conscious of their homosexuality, may feel the need for a wife in terms of their business or professional careers. The married business man is often in a better position for advancement. Some of America's most prestigious corporations are apprehensive about letting the unmarried man reach top executive level—too often he is conceived as a risk. Professional men too, especially those in the Church or in education, realize that they will be safer if they are married. It can also be said that since homosexual persons are banned from some vocations, such as the military and the Church, men, knowing full well what their sexual orientation is, may get married to construct, if it is not too harsh to say, a "smoke screen" which will provide protection.

Sixthly, homosexual men may marry because they love the women they marry and also want to enjoy relating to, living with, being emotionally supported by a woman. *Charles Laughton: An Intimate Biography,* by Charles Higham (Doubleday, 1976), the recently published biography of one of Hollywood's greats, tells of the long years of sharing, which he and Elsa Lanchester knew as husband and wife—yet for almost all the years of his marriage he was homosexual, had a series of men with whom he was involved, and in some instances established deep, long-term relationships with them.

In the final analysis it cannot be categorically said that men with a homosexual orientation should not marry. That he and his wife may have to face problems that arise out of his homosexuality can be hardly denied. I would hope that the material in this chapter will indicate that many uncompromising, destructive, and fragmenting decisions can be avoided, or at least modified, when there is a wife or other family members who can be empathetic, sensitive, and caring.

6

Emily–A Gay Wife

Dear George

Are you surprised at receiving a letter from me? I
wonder if you have forgotten that on the day we finally
separated I promised I would let you know at the end
of a year how I feel about us and how I've managed to
adjust to my life with Janet. Well, since that year ended
yesterday, I thought I'd fulfill my promise and write. I
know that we've seen each other these last few months
when you've come to take the children, but there have
never been moments when we could sit down together
by ourselves.

I think I've made a right decision, George. I think
it's right for me, for you; I also hope my decision has
been good for Janet and the children. A year may not
seem like a long time; on the other hand I do feel that
this has been one of the most important years of my
life.

Oh, everything has not been a bed of roses. Janet
and I have had our own hard moments. She has not
found it easy adjusting to the children, but this is
getting better and I do believe that Rob and Judy
(especially Rob) are growing closer to her. Finances
have been strained at times, but now that Rob has
started first grade and Judy is in a good nursery
school, my part-time job is relieving the situation.

I wish I could stop feeling guilty—this is one of my
great problems. First of all, I still feel badly about us.
As I tried to say over and over again I did marry you

because I felt I loved you. I had every intention of
making our marriage work. Surely you know as well as
I do that it wasn't a perfect marriage (When is one
perfect?). I think we both know we were too young and
too immature. If you are honest I think you'll have to
admit that your heavy drinking at times didn't help our
situation, but now that I understand more about
myself, I can sense some of the pain you may have
been feeling and why the drinking took place. I know
I've upset your life badly, George, and for this, I am
sorry. I just have to feel that in the long run you will
find a new life which can end up being far more
satisfactory for you.

I guess I also feel guilty about both our parents. I
presume it will always be difficult for them to
understand. Fortunately, they seem to feel a little
better about things, at least your mother does call now
and again to ask about the children. Perhaps in the
summer they could visit with her.

Frankly I don't know whether to feel guilty about the
children or not. I have mixed emotions. It may be that
the ideal home environment for a child has a man in it.
Nevertheless, we all know of well-adjusted, responsible
adults who have grown up in single-sex homes. There
are widows and even unmarried women who have
brought up children and done a good job. Children
can find adequate male models outside the home. In
our case, Rob and Judy do have a father, and I'm glad
you care about them. I know they love you; I hope
they always will. Even though a man does not live in
our home, even though you and I are separated, I am
tempted to believe that perhaps it is better for them to
be in an environment where there isn't the tension,
fighting, and bickering which marked our last months
together. This is hard for everyone concerned. Things
are quieter here, and for this I'm glad.

I would be ducking the issue if I said I wasn't
worried about what happens in a few years when both
children are farther along in school and they begin to
wonder what the real relationship is between Janet and

me. Schoolmates can be cruel, and society in general has not learned to look too charitably upon persons like Janet and me. I don't know how to deal with this. I've just decided not to worry at this moment and let each day take care of itself.

George, I said that in a year I'd let you know about our getting a divorce. In many ways divorce or no divorce does not affect me. Now, it's what may seem best for you. If you want to go ahead, all right. I think I've had time enough to know that this is where I need to be for the sake of my own inner self; I am fully convinced that you and I can't begin over again. I rather sense you feel the same way. I do respect you enough and care enough that I hope your life, too, will find some new direction so that you will have what you need and what you deserve.

This is a longer letter than I intended but I guess I just wanted to get these thoughts in a bit of order. Thank you for your patience. I'll probably see you on Saturday when you come for the children.

Emily

On the day Emily left her home and moved with the children into Janet's apartment, one can try to imagine the conversation that took place in the home of her own parents.

Mother: I never believed Emily would do it.

Father: Well, you ought to know that she's always been strong headed.

Mother: Yes, but to actually go ahead with this. I still can't understand.

Father: George always seemed a decent guy. Sure, they had their quarrels and differences, but I don't see why they couldn't stick it out at least for the sake of the children.

Mother: She says they did go for counseling but it didn't help very much. In fact she said the counselor thought that maybe some temporary separation might be best.

Father: But what I really can't understand is why she'd leave George to live with a woman. It's one thing if she got involved with a man, but this other business doesn't make much sense to me.

Mother: I guess I can't figure that one out very well myself. All she seems to tell me is that she and Janet have lots of things in common. Janet likes the children, and she believes it will be better if the children don't have to live with all the fighting that went on between her and George.

Father: That may be true, but I still think she's made a serious mistake.

Mother: Maybe there's lots more to this than we know. She did admit that she and George weren't happy together in the bed; in fact, they'd stopped having sex a long time ago. Maybe that's why he was so mad all the time.

Father: Perhaps Emily's a lezzie.

Mother: Don't say that! How do you know anything about such things?

Emily's situation is not as rare as it might sound. Hers is a story of latent homosexuality which develops, "blossoms," after a few years of marriage. From a clinical point of view, considering what has already been said about the establishment of sexual identity, it has to be stated that her basic sexual orientation is homosexual and has been since early years. However, for a whole series of reasons this realization does not overtake her until many other things have happened in her life. A closer look at Emily's story reveals more facts.

As a girl and as a young woman she saw herself as a wife and mother. She was not highly motivated about getting an education or building a career. She did go on to college but dropped out at the end of her first year. By nature she has always been an emotional person who needed physical contact and affection. Being attractive, it was never difficult to win the attention of the opposite sex. Boys were always wanting to date her and she had been sexually involved before she finally met George.

Girls who want a home and children try to choose the right

husband. George had finished college and had started a good job in his father's business. He seemed industrious and ambitious. He came from a good family that seemed on a social par with her own. He said he loved her and was most eager that she marry him.

Weddings are important to most girls. She had fantasized hers for a long time. She wanted all the traditional trappings, and her family was in a position to provide them. There were the showers, the wedding preparations, the rehearsal dinner, the church, the bridesmaids, the country club reception, the Bermuda honeymoon. What more could a girl ask?

The marriage started off well. His parents had helped with a down payment on their ranch house. Wedding gifts and furniture from her family made the home comfortable and attractive. She and George seemed to be communicating well. The only problem that was emerging was their sexual relationship. It seemed O.K. at first, but George was more demanding than she felt was fair. He began to be more and more aggressive; at times he even seemed sadistic. He seemed angry and frustrated because she was making it clear that she wasn't enjoying their sex. More and more she was finding excuses not to sleep with him; often she feigned physical symptoms. She began to think she needed to talk with someone about her problems, but she couldn't muster the courage. She was sure that George would not go with her for help. She delayed.

George's drinking seemed to increase. It didn't affect his work, but he began to be more critical of her and became abusive at times. His patience with the children occasionally wore quite thin. Emily began to raise some doubts in her own mind about the future of her marriage. It was about this time that Janet came into her life.

Janet was about two years younger. She had already finished her nursing training and worked on the staff of the local hospital. They met at a neighborhood party at which the hostess was displaying and selling some attractive copper items. There was something rather shy and sensitive about Janet; Emily was usually effervescent and outgoing. She often noticed quiet people at parties and would make some effort to reach out to them. She liked Janet from the start. Since they did not live far apart, Janet offered to drop Emily home and spare George the special trip to collect her. As they chatted, it turned out they shopped at the same supermarket. Since Janet worked the 11:00 P.M., to 7:00 A.M. shift at the hospital, she offered to pick up Emily some mid-morning to take her shopping. Emily said she would phone. A couple of days later she did, and after the shopping trip Janet came in for coffee. And this is how it all began.

Little by little Emily felt herself drawn to Janet. She did not seem to know why. There was something about Janet, perhaps because she was a nurse and had real care for and interest in people—especially those in pain—which made it possible for her to talk about herself, to discuss her relationship with George, even to indicate that she was more and more unhappy about the marriage. Emily was also beginning to sense that Janet was being warmer, more open with her. She had wondered why Janet, an attractive young woman, hadn't married and didn't seem to be interested in dating men. She was careful not to probe too deeply or to ask too many direct personal questions.

One morning when they had arranged to go shopping, Emily telephoned Janet to say she didn't feel well and in fact had gone back to bed after getting George off to work. Janet offered to stop by to see if there was anything she could do; after all she was a nurse. The door was unlocked, so she went directly to the bedroom. She sat down on the edge of the bed, she felt Emily's brow, and then took her hand. Something happened in this moment of touching. They have said this was the moment they knew that they loved each other. From this morning on there seemed no way of turning back.

Now Janet was able to talk about herself. She said she had always known that she was homosexual. Growing up that way had been difficult. She had to hide it from everyone. She was an only child, and as a young girl she loved to have other girls visit and stay overnight. She was especially happy when they could sleep together. Sometimes there were those she could "cuddle with." Boys just didn't interest her. In high school when the rest of the girls seemed to talk constantly about their dates, she said little or occasionally manufactured some story. Her sexual life seemed dormant. When she went into nursing school, however, she did find a classmate who apparently had some of the same feelings she had known. They grew closer to the extent that they finally shared their "secret" together. A physical, sexual relationship started, but they had to be unusually cautious because of the school authorities. They did have some special times when they shared a few holidays together in Janet's home. Graduation separated them. Her friend had family obligations which caused her return to the Midwest. Correspondence continued for awhile, but time and distance made it impossible for them to make any plans, and now the affair was really, for all intents and purposes, ended.

And so the months passed by. Emily and Janet's relationship deepened. It grew more and more serious. Janet's working schedule, their living proximity, and the fact that Janet could help Emily in the mornings with shopping, housework, and care of the children made it natural and easy for them to be together without the undue suspicions of neighbors or without George or any of the parents involved growing apprehensive.

Emily was beginning to panic. How could all this be happening to her? She needed to talk with someone. Perhaps she had better seek professional help. Her family physician had known her since she was born. She believed she could trust him. He was kind, yet sorry her marriage was in trouble and distressed that she had become involved in a lesbian relationship. He frankly admitted he did not know very much about homosexuality but would try and discover if he could find a therapist in the community who did. He called her the next morning with the name of a clinical psychologist, a woman who had done considerable study on human sexuality as she prepared for her Ph.D. She was reputed to be knowledgeable about homosexuality. Emily made an appointment.

It took only a few sessions for this therapist to uncover

Emily's true sexuality and to help her see how her homosexual orientation had lain below the surface for all her years. The counselor would make no prognosis in terms of whether some therapies might bring about some sexual reorientation. She admitted that she did not know any successful techniques. She said that if Emily were interested in following through with another therapist that she would try to provide some name or names. The doctor did suggest, however, that she and George try to find someone for marriage counseling, not necessarily with the hope of saving the marriage but of working through the difficulty in which they now found themselves. The counselor would not tell her whether she should or should not tell George the whole truth, nor would she make any specific suggestions as to how Emily and Janet were going to work out their hopes of living together.

Taking her counselor's advice, she followed through by discussing with George their need for some counseling. Although not too happy with the idea, he had begun to realize that the marriage seemed to be reaching an impasse. Emily had moved further and further away from him. They quarreled more and more. She was even irritated when he tried to put his arms around her. He realized he was drinking too much each night. He was still chagrined that he had gotten so furious that he'd said some really nasty things to her and even pushed her. An honest appraisal made him feel that the situation might get worse before it got better. They went to a counselor together. They saw the counselor separately. Emily had been honest with the counselor in her individual session. The counselor agreed that a trial separation might be wise.

During this period Janet moved from her parents' home and found a two-bedroom apartment. When the moment came for the break, Emily said that Janet offered her a place for a while at least. The children could also go with her. George still did not know the real truth. Emily could not bring herself to tell him; neither could she tell her parents. George had suggested that she stay in their home and he would move; but Emily and Janet knew this wouldn't work since it would look strange if Janet moved in with her. And so the plan was for her and the children to move in with Janet.

George and Emily's parting was not too pleasant. He was angry, felt rejected, was filled with feelings of inadequacy and saw a lonely road ahead. However, he said he would wait a year before filing for a divorce, and he made it clear he wanted to see the children on a regular basis. He agreed to help with the financial care of the children but he was not in any mood to provide her with money. She would have to go to work or get help from her parents.

As the year moved along, George's bitterness seemed to moderate. Gradually he began to realize what the relationship between Emily and Janet was. He was shaken at first—his male ego was hurt, he reacted like many other men to lesbians— how can women prefer women when men are available? But as he sensed Emily's happiness, as he began to know Janet and respect her as a person, as he realized that the two women really loved the children and made a good home for them, he tempered his attitude considerably. He even reached the point that when he brought the children back on his day with them, he could stop for a drink. A couple of times he stayed on for supper. Yes, hard though it was to face the reality, Emily seemed to have found the right person with whom to share her life. She did have a new radiancy, a new interest in the world around her, and she was finding new purposes for her life. She was still a good mother. He felt he should let her have her life. Soon he would talk with her about the divorce.

7

Gordon – A Gay Father

Dear Carol and Jeff,

First of all I do send love to you and your households. Being your father I am obviously comforted that each of you has your own family now and that things apparently go well for you. The only distress I feel is that we now live so far apart it is difficult to have our family reunions and more opportunity to be together. However, letters become at least one way for us to keep in touch. The letter I am now writing should have been written some time ago, but since it is a difficult one to write, I have continued to put it off until another time.

I am quite aware that you have had a number of questions about what is going on with our plans at home and we have not given you much information. Now that the future is shaping up, we want you to know what is happening.

Our plans are these: Our house has been sold to a family from St. Louis. We have put a deposit on a condominium in Alexandria to reinvest the money that we gain from the sale of the house. Mom will be moving there by the end of the month. I have rented an apartment in Washington and have begun living there during the week most of the time.

This means that Mom and I are living separately. You are aware, I am sure, of some of the strains that there have been in our relationship, especially in the past few years. The main problem is my sexual orientation which is bisexual and, possibly more correctly, homosexual. This is something that I have lived with all of my adult life and have tried to hide during my married years. For the past two years Mom has known the truth about me, but she had suspected it for many years. In many ways it is a relief to me to know that the family is aware of my situation, and yet living with it is difficult for a married couple. Therefore, if I am going to be honest with myself and with others, it is perhaps best that we try living separately at least most of the time.

May I assure you that I still love Mom very much. I am sorry for the hurt I have caused her and you during these many years. I am most sorry for the deception which seemed to me to be the best way to handle it, but which was perhaps unfair to everyone.

What the future holds for us, we are not sure. Maybe it can all be resolved happily for everyone. I hope so. At any rate we are trying to live our lives honestly and openly, trusting that our children will understand and appreciate our plight. No matter what happens, I ask for your love and respect and for your prayers that God will guide us to the right goals for our lives.

I would welcome the opportunity to discuss this with you by letter or phone or, most importantly, face to face, as I have with your sister, Anne, since she has been living with us this past year. I hope we can do this soon. I am sending this letter on to Mom and she will have an opportunity to add her note and send it on to you.

I love you all very much.

Love,
Dad

In my years of counseling, I cannot recall a single person, either a youth or an adult, contacting me because of distress over having a gay parent. As previous chapters indicate, parents have been anxious about their children, sisters and brothers have been upset, husbands and wives have sought help. I wonder what it means that persons have not come to say "Dad is gay" or "Mom is gay."

I am tempted to suggest that since the majority of sons and daughters who might be having to deal with the homosexuality of a parent would be under twenty-five, the chances are that they will have responses that are far more liberal than those of a prior generation. Twenty years ago the word homosexuality was still being whispered. There was little open discussion and only a minimal amount of information available. The picture has changed radically. There has been law change in many states removing homosexual acts from the criminal code (providing there is no duress, no affront to public decency, and that persons involved have reached the age of sexual consent); Civil Rights Acts have been adopted in several municipalities to protect homosexual persons, especially in terms of employment and housing; prominent men and women have openly admitted their homosexual orientation; supportive editorials and articles appear in newspapers and national magazines; popular television talk shows air the subject; gay caucuses are emerging within major professional organizations and societies; gay groups have established themselves within many major Christian denominations, and even a fast-growing, far-reaching Church, basically involving gays, continues to grow in strength. Young people who have been exposed to this changing scene have developed an understanding, a tolerance, even an acceptance of homosexual persons that is perhaps unprecedented in any previous period of history. Therefore, the knowledge they may have that a parent is gay is not necessarily earth shattering; at least the pain doesn't seem great enough for them to rush off for professional counseling help.

Coupled with this more liberal attitude about homosexuality is youth's own attitude about sex in general. Young people today are more enlightened on the subject than those only a few years their seniors. Instruction about sex is taking place in some school systems, colleges now offer survey courses. Christian denominations, especially the Unitarian-Universalist Church, have developed helpful programs, and organizations such as SIECUS and Planned Parenthood distribute highly creditable material for youth. Children learn earlier about their bodies, their sexual organs, and about conception, pregnancy, and birth. Masturbation is being removed as a threat to mental and physical health; in the minds of many Christian moralists it is no longer a sin. Whether the Church or society in general is offering full approval of genital relationships before marriage, statistics seem to verify that the incidence is higher with each passing year. There is enough knowledge abroad to indicate that bisexuality may be known to more people than was once realized so that sexual encounter with both sexes does not necessarily mean that some homosexual experience is evidence of a fixed sexual orientation.

It is not only in things sexual that young people today are more liberal, but there are also other areas where this is true. The prejudices once known toward persons because of race, skin color, national origin, religious affiliation have been greatly reduced. Young people seem more tolerant of another's political, social, and economic stance. There is a wider range in terms of clothes, social conduct, and life-style. Therefore, in this light it may become clearer why parents may get considerably exercised about their children's homosexuality; while, in contrast, young people are not overly distressed nor censorious when the truth is made clear that a parent is gay.

Strangely enough, gay parents may be the last persons to expect or hope for acceptance from their children. They may manage to unburden themselves to many others before they finally find the courage to open up to their children. Apparently such is the case with Gordon, the "Dad" who has addressed the letter to "Carol and Jeff." He has been sharing the problem with his wife, he probably has been in counseling, he may have made this clear to friends and other associates. Since she was living at home, it would seem he had to be honest with Anne, but the others, who seem to live at some distance, are left to the last. He knows he should have written earlier but "another time" always seemed better.

I suspect that there are few children who do not, as they

grow up, wonder what the actual sexual relationship may be
between their parents. Are the parents sexually compatible?
Have they enjoyed their sex together? Do they still do it? As
young people know their own sexual needs and recognize the
drives within them, they may wonder about how long these will
last. Sometimes I am suspicious that young people act out
sexually so often because they have some idea that it is better
"to get as much as you can" before it's too late. They are apt
to hear stories about impotency, frigidity, loss of libido, and
malfunctioning which come with increasing age, and they
worry about their own sexual futures. They think about their
parents and try to imagine them as sexual persons. Obviously
they don't ask; they just have to guess.

I hope I'm not wrong in believing that the majority of children will be pleased and encouraged if they can know that
their parents are still enjoying an adequate, satisfactory sexual
life together. They may very well want to make their own
identification with it. By this I mean they deduce that "if they
are doing it at their age, maybe I'll manage, too!" It seems only
fair to say that children are happiest when they know their
parents still love each other, when their relationship is still full
of life, and when their bedrooms can be a comfortable sanctuary. But children are usually realists. They have learned early
the complex ties of human relationships. They may be able to
understand and to accept, more than we ever suspect, that
parents must cope with their own evolving and changing personalities, that one or the other may develop a new relationship outside the marriage, that even divorce and remarriage
may take place. This is a phenomenon that they may be able
to take in stride. To say that they may not be hurt, to believe
that children wouldn't want it some other way, would not be
realistic. It would also be out of the ordinary for children not
only to make adjustment to these situations but they might
very well adopt the attitude that parents have a right to know
and experience what is best for them.

There is another point to be raised here. Children are
often far more sensitive than parents suspect. It is probably

true to say that no child ever truly understands the real relationship which exists between the parents. (In reality how can any of us understand fully the dynamic which marks the bond between two human beings?) Still, children have some idea of how parents feel toward each other. The incidence of quarrels, harsh words, or even physical confrontations does not necessarily indicate that parents don't love each other. In contrast, just because two people manage to live together peacefully, with a certain kind of surface congeniality, and even an expressed care for each other, is not proof that their love is alive, that they are still attracted to each other, that they are meeting their sexual needs with each other. For myriad reasons, they are living together, acting out their marriage. Children who love their parents, who see them as persons, who would want them to continue to enjoy fulfilled lives, cannot be happy with the "dead" marriage in which their parents may be living.

This brings us to Gordon and his letter to Carol and Jeff. What will they write back to their father? Or what will they say if, as he suggests, they find some opportunity to converse face to face? His letter makes it clear that he and "Mom" have already dealt with the matter and have made some practical plans which are sensible to both of them. It is clear that his wife has known of his homosexuality for some time; apparently she has been suffering quietly. Gordon is in pain about all this— sorry that he has hurt his wife; distressed that he must ask his children to cope with his problem. He is honest in indicating that his homosexuality did not suddenly appear and, that he has wrestled with this proclivity for many years. He has had to hide, to be deceptive, to try and live in two worlds. The children are now grown, educated, and some are married. The family financial picture is secure enough. The time has now come for him to be honest with himself and with those he loves. He must risk their possible censure or rejection. He makes it clear in spite of all that he loves his family. Surely it would be his hope that they will understand and continue to love him.

One cannot always guess how people will respond to stressful situations. If Carol and Jeff have not had any previous hints of their father's homosexuality, this letter could be a very real shock. They apparently do know that, at least in recent years, the marriage has had its own strains. They may be somewhat prepared that a separation might take place. The reason for the breakup of the home will be the most difficult one they must try to handle. In consideration of some of the points already raised in this chapter, is there not some chance they will be understanding, forgiving, and willing to assure their father that he will not be abandoned? They are young and perhaps liberal; they don't want their parents to live in a strained, uncomfortable, false marriage. They are glad that Dad has said he still loves Mother, that he is concerned about her future, that he is providing for her financially. They are encouraged that he has already shared this with Anne. It would seem that he is still maintaining his career and has found a comfortable place in which to live. It would appear that he has every hope and expectation of keeping contact with the family. What gain will there be if they reject him? They can sense the pain and suffering he has already had to bear. If they write or if they see him will it not be best for all concerned if they tell him they do understand? He has been a good Dad; won't he still be?

The question has been raised in previous chapters as to why persons who are homosexual end up in heterosexual marriages. It is not difficult to find a few answers. In some situations, as made clear in the story of Emily which comprises the previous chapter, hers was a latent homosexuality. It is my contention that such can occur more frequently with women than with men. I do believe that most men have a fairly clear picture of what their real sexual feelings are quite early in their maturing process, most surely by the time when they are generally contemplating marriage. However, room must always be made for exceptions. Some men may well know of their sexual identity, but as already has been said, they prefer to deny it, to talk themselves out of it, and to anticipate the possibility that a marriage will obliterate their homosexual desires. Collected evidence does not seem to substantiate such a hope. It is even my contention that almost the reverse takes place in the sense that those who have held back from genital sex because of their homosexuality discover when they become active heterosexually that the drive to be involved homosexually only grows sharper and more demanding. And secondly, although they may function successfully with their wives in the early years of marriage so that they control homosexual urges, that as their sexual drive begins to reduce, the stronger homosexual inclination increases so that their potency with their wives diminishes while they can manage adequately in a homosexual encounter.

The reader must be reminded that although persons may be homosexual, this does not negate their paternal or maternal feelings. For this reason homosexual men and women may marry. Is this wise? Is this fair? Well, it has to be stated that should such men or women openly announce their sexual orientation, what would be their chances, considering the present social climate, of being allowed to adopt a child or children? It is true there are isolated cases of single persons being allowed to adopt, and some may very well be homosexual, but I sincerely doubt that the agency personnel held responsible for such matters are aware that the adopting parent is homosexual. Until learning otherwise, I will have to believe that state departments charged with the care and protection of children are not knowingly placing their children in foster homes where those providing parental care are considered to be homosexual. Single men and women are looked upon with a certain suspicion if they want to work with youth organizations like scouting, YMCA/YWCA, Big Brotherhood, and Church youth groups. If they do get an opportunity to volunteer, they are often watched very carefully. The result is that these homosexual single persons may be particularly careful to avoid any overidentification with a particular boy or girl. Single teachers as well as single clergy (with the exception of those who are expected to be living the rules of celibacy) cause questions to be raised in people's minds as to whether or not they may be homosexual.

The net result of all this is that it does appear that society is not ready to grant the homosexual person the privilege of being paternal or maternal. Since marriage may not be wise, few options are open. Even adoption is seldom possible. This paternal need and the desire to have some constructive influence upon the life of a growing child had at least one flowering moment in history wherein there was not merely acceptance but even some social pressure that adult men meet such an obligation. This was in classical Greece in that period referred to as the Golden Age. It became the duty of a male citizen to "adopt" a Greek boy, probably about fourteen, and see that he learn citizenship, philosophy, arms-bearing, and all the other things a Greek male was expected to know. Mary Renault's sensitive novel *The Last of the Wine* provides historical information about these Greek relationships.

The fact that men throughout the passing centuries have wanted to be part of the lives of developing boys can be adequately substantiated. A volume, *Greek Love,* by E. G. Eglington, follows this theme through history since the days of Plato and Socrates. The author makes it clear that ever since this Grecian period, such man-boy relationships have not only endured but also have been a positive influence in the lives of the boys involved. At the end of his book Eglington cites fifty contemporary case histories in which boys lacking proper father figures have found useful places in society because a surrogate father, who may have been homosexual, helped them grow into responsible manhood.

Because there are isolated instances when homosexual persons, some of them emotionally ill and immoral, do not fulfill their duties faithfully and responsibly when they have youth in their charge, with the result that there are incidents of bizarre antisocial activities (usually well publicized in print), the general public is apt to take the position that all homosexuals will act this way. Therefore it seems wiser to keep all homosexuals away from children and youth. To counter this, is it not fair to say it is inconsistent reasoning because there are numerous scandals which involve heterosexual persons acting improperly with children? Child abuse is a growing national concern; it is usually taking place within the family and is generally perpetrated by natural fathers and mothers.

I cannot know what the experience of other counselors may be, but I can say without reservation that in situations in which one parent of the family is homosexual, I have not found that this person has been irresponsible. At times, the homosexual parent, male or female, has been the more caring parent. No such parent has indicated that he or she did not want to continue contact with the children. Over and over again, the pain they have borne if a separation has or will take place, is that of no longer having the close, continuing care for the child. Homosexual parents of both sexes often go to great lengths, even into court, to try to win custody of their children if they feel convinced they can provide the best care. I have had to be involved in several such court situations (always painful, to my mind), and I have heard older children, when asked by the judge to indicate their own choice of a living situation, to opt to be with the homosexual parent.

What information do we have to support the contention that gay parents can be good parents? The best proof of this perhaps has to come from the children themselves. Obviously young children or even young adults are not producing books or writing articles which can underscore such an observation. Adults who have known about the homosexuality of a parent might produce some evidence, but at this writing I cannot think of any essays or articles with the title "My Father is Gay" or "My Mother is a Lesbian." Children seem quite careful about revealing the homosexual identity of a parent. Considering the social climate, which is still negative about homosexuality, persons may not want to embarrass a parent, may not want to open themselves up to ridicule. Or they may feel they are overstepping their bounds in terms of the position other members of the family—grandparents, brothers and sisters, aunts and uncles—have taken. The question of whether the gay parent is living or deceased would hardly change the situation.

In this connection I do recall one conference held in New York City under the sponsorship of the Homosexual Community Counseling Center at which there was a panel of five or six persons—between the ages of about 18 and 30—who, not homosexual themselves, admitted in that professional environment that one of their parents could be identified as gay. Not one was negative about the gay parents. I still remember a couple of responses. One woman openly explained that her mother was lesbian and that when the children were teenagers had entered into a relationship with another woman. It was with her mother's lover that this young woman had one of her most meaningful relationships. She felt a close bond with her and managed to communicate with her better than she could with her own parents. A second panelist who was one of several children said "Oh, we all knew Daddy was gay so we left the matter alone. He was a good father and we all loved him."

There is one final point to raise in this chapter.

If a parent is gay, then isn't there a strong possibility this will affect the children in the family so that a child may become homosexual. If one should ever accede to this comment, then how does one respond to the fact that it is generally taken for granted that all homosexual persons have heterosexual parents? Straight parents are apparently not trying to teach their children to be homosexual. As has been noted in previous chapters, the etiology of homosexuality is still shrouded in mystery. No one can say that it is taught or caught; it doesn't seem to be hereditary or hormonal; no final conclusion can be made that it is because the parent did this or did that; no single sexual experience or series of experiences seems to bring about such an orientation. We may do well to ascribe to the belief of many authorities on sexual identity that at this point in history no one knows for sure why anyone, heterosexual, bisexual, or homosexual has the feelings which make up his or her sexual orientation. It is difficult to perceive why any homosexual parent would want a son or daughter to be gay or who would make any effort (if such were possible) to have this happen. Gay parents are too familiar with the pain, the trauma, of being homosexual to want their children to bear the difficulties their homosexuality has brought to them.

8

Gary–A Gay Teacher

Dear Norman:

Last weekend was just great. I needed that chance to get away for a few hours. Thank God this term is getting near the end; I don't think I can stand the kids much longer and I presume they feel the same about me. I imagine you're looking forward to your final classes, too.

Your place at the lake is surely a beautiful spot. No doubt you've been glad over the years you decided to buy it. I just wish you lived a little nearer so we could see each other more often, but that's a long drive especially on Friday and Sunday nights when the traffic is heavy.

You may remember that I promised to let you know whether anything came of my running into one of my pupils at the bar a couple of weeks ago. You're lucky it never happened to you, but I guess you can be glad the drinking age in your state still stands at twenty-one; since ours is reduced to eighteen you never know who in the devil is going to be at the Blue Door or Dominic's.

I can tell you those were a few tense minutes when I spotted him; he was with a couple of older chaps I didn't know. I think I saw him first. I guess my immediate response was to just bolt. On the other hand, I thought that might be awkward if he's already seen me or should see me dash out. He's really a decent fellow and graduates in June. I had him for geometry last year and I felt he thought me O.K. He was a good student and no problem in class. I must say I never expected to see him in the Blue Door. But as you might guess that bar continues to be full of surprises.

As I told you, I didn't know whether to speak to him or not. The problem was solved when he needed to go to the john and he had to pass me. He stopped, said "Hello, Mr. Drake, glad to see you again," and then went along. We made a bit of small conversation when he passed by to return to his friends.

Well, I can tell you I didn't sleep very well that night. What might that chap do? After all, I argued with myself, he was in a gay bar and I'm darned sure he knew where he was. Whether he and the guys he was with were gay or were just gawking, I can hardly know. There was the possibility he could report to the principal, which might end a fourteen-year teaching career. However, I honestly felt he wouldn't do that. He could tell a teacher or two, but I even doubted that. The thing I really feared was his talking with the other kids and some nasty rumors getting started. Well, thank God, nothing has happened. In fact, on Tuesday we passed in the hall and he smiled and spoke very cordially. I think as we looked at each other I heard us saying, without words, "If you don't tell on me, I won't tell on you!"

I guess, Norm, this was a rather narrow one and it makes me nervous. I don't feel quite as comfortable at the Blue Door now so I think I may stay away. I'll wait until weekends when I can get into the city.

Hope you'll have a good summer. My plans are still up in the air. Perhaps we can get in a visit before you fly off to Spain.

Cheers!
Gary

Some social scientists have believed that over the past few years we have been living in a new age of enlightenment.

Points can be made to support this as one thinks about the Civil Rights Movement and Gay Pride. More and more barriers seem to be breaking down so that there is new freedom, new opportunity for many. The homophile movement is a relatively recent one and it has made remarkable strides. In the minds of some it has gone further and moved faster than its earliest supporters dared hope. But a long road lies ahead, and on the way there may be some serious land slides to block the way so that some tortuous detours may be unavoidable.

Although more than a third of the states have now passed, in one form or another, sexual consent laws which basically remove genital acts between members of the same sex from the criminal code, no state has yet passed legislation which will protect persons' civil rights regardless of sexual orientation or affectional preference. Such bills have been introduced into state assemblies, but none have managed to pass. Clearance is often possible through proper committees charged with concern for human rights, but when debate takes place, lawmakers are pressured by some politically important groups so that passage of such bills has been impossible. Many states have civil rights laws protecting persons in housing, employment, and public accommodations regardless of color, race, national origin, sex, religion, and so on. Those sympathetic with the plight of gay people in this area merely want to add the words "regardless of sexual orientation." At present there are efforts to have Congress pass such a bill.

What forces are generating the greatest resistance? Two: the Church and those who are opposed to the employment of homosexual teachers. It is not difficult to conceive why there are some Christian denominations that feel they cannot be supportive. As homophile leaders point out that the Church is an institution which constantly preaches freedom, justice, liberty, equality, yet in this area it is restrictive and prohibiting.

The fear of the gay teacher is really the biggest problem in terms of gay rights legislation. There are certain teacher associations, especially organizations of principals and administrators, which will register their negative attitude. Principals and superintendents say they don't want to be in a position where they are forced to hire a known gay teacher; secondly they want to be free to dismiss a teacher if they discover the teacher is homosexual. Some teachers openly say they don't want to have to teach with or be associated with homosexuals. They can have no respect for them and are fully convinced they should not be allowed to influence children and young people. In all fairness it does have to be said that certain educational associations have taken a favorable position on such bills.

In the long run the greatest pressure comes from the parents themselves. Their indoctrination over the years—that gay people molest children, poison their minds, will be like the Pied Piper leading them into a life-style which is perverse, unnatural, and immoral—has been so great that any change of mind and heart cannot come suddenly but must be realized through the slow process of education, more education, and more education.

I will be repeating arguments already presented if I rehearse the support one can build for making such statements as: We can't know for sure why persons are homosexual, bisexual, or heterosexual. Homosexuals do not become such through isolated sexual incidents. Homosexuals cannot be termed child molesters. Gay people have known so much pain in their lives that they would not try to win others (if they could) to their particular sexual persuasion. Homosexual men and women have often had deep, positive, abiding influences on the lives of growing maturing children and young people.

In the years of my counseling, a large percentage of those who have sought help are from the various professions. I don't claim an accurate statistic, but I do believe that the largest number would fall in the field of teaching. In my mind these have been fine, conscientious, committed men and women. I can think of no single incident where one has been sexually involved or emotionally attached to a pupil. Because they have realized they are vulnerable to suspicion, to gossip, and even to dismissal they have probably been overcautious. Outside of

their classrooms they have often worked in educational programs for community youth organizations and churches. In
summer periods many have served on camp and conference
staffs and have had direct relationship to young people. They
have possessed high moral value systems, they have fulfilled
their duties effectively, and they have not been any embarrassment to staff leaders or administrative personnel.

I am confident that few school systems are without gay
teachers. Obviously they are not identified as gay; possibly
some of their fellow teachers or even an occasional member
of the administration may know, but beyond that they usually
must stay hidden. Once at an open hearing before a state
legislative committee, prior to the introduction of a civil rights
bill, a statement was made to the effect that if every gay teacher
in that state suddenly resigned or was discharged, the entire
school system of the state might be in danger of collapse.

What are gay teachers like? What are their special problems?
Well, there is Gary, whose letter opens this chapter, and then
there is Maureen, a lesbian. Their life-styles are quite different.

Gary is in his mid- to late-thirties. Early in his college years
he made his decision to teach. He went right on for his master's degree and after three years of teaching he earned his
sixth year certificate which meant thirty added credits. Since
he felt committed to high school teaching he did not feel
motivated to undertake a doctoral program.

He was born in a small town in the New England Berkshires.
He had a brother eight years older who was killed in a motorcycle accident before Gary finished elementary school. This
was a tragedy for the whole family and, as far as he was concerned, made his parents particularly conscious of his well
being. He felt they became overprotective: No motorcycle for
him, and his mother especially seemed to worry about him. In
his later years he wondered if this kind of solicitous care had
anything to do with his being homosexual. He was never natu-
rally drawn to the usual sports although he did swim, enjoyed
basketball to some extent, and did follow through in scouting

until he earned his Eagle badge. He also seemed to have a musical talent and took piano lessons until he was in his middle high school years. With some financial sacrifice the family was able to grant his wish to go to a small private Eastern college which he felt had a strong mathematics department. He went to Boston to finish his master's degree.

Gary lived a sheltered, rather narrow life in his home community. It was a place where everybody seemed to know everyone else. As he began to discover his sexual feelings, he was troubled that he seemed different. He did not necessarily enjoy talking about sex with girls as his buddies did. He made friends with girls but never seemed to want to get serious. During some of his camping experiences as a scout there had been some horse play which got sexual a few times; but these experiences seemed rather embarrassing to him. In high school he began to feel some strong attractions to other males, especially the handsome athletic ones, but he was very careful of his conduct because he didn't ever want to be identified with a couple of effeminate boys who were always being teased and called "queers."

A small college is also a small town. Gossip is ever present. Campus gay movements had not really crystallized at this time —surely not at his conservative alma mater. By now he had begun to do some reading; he became more and more convinced he might very well be homosexual. He was worried, but not so much that his studies suffered. He did find some good friends and managed a comfortable enough social life.

It was at graduate school that he knew the time had come to deal with his sexuality. Boston is a big city. It is easy to get lost, to be anonymous. He had heard about gay bars, about cruising areas. With some trepidation he entered his first gay bar. It was about as frightening as he expected it to be. He gulped down one drink, spoke to no one and bolted out. But he had seen enough to intrigue him. It was a place where people seemed to be visiting, to be laughing. There were certainly some good-looking guys there—the majority seemed about his age. He went back. This was the beginning of his involvement in Boston's gay life. There were affairs now and again. He found a small circle of gay friends. He even went through the trauma of a gay love affair which, when it had a dramatic ending, disturbed him enough so that he sought help through a counseling service especially aimed at assisting persons who are homosexual. His weeks with a therapist helped him understand himself better, to provide some basic self-acceptance, and to get a few priorities in order if he were going to move into a teaching career in a medium-sized New England city where the board of education had made him a decent offer.

His teaching record of fourteen years has been a fine one. He is cooperative with the administration, gets along with fellow teachers, and seems to have the respect of students. He has little trouble with discipline. Because he is single he has not developed an active outside social life with the married teachers. He has become identified with a local church and works on some of its committees. He has a few friends who share his interest in music, and they attend various community concerts or may travel to other nearby communities for such events. Little by little he has found a circle of gay friends so that there is an occasional dinner, Sunday brunch, or cocktail party. He often goes back home weekends since his mother and father are getting older and they enjoy his visits. His small city can boast only a couple of rather quiet sedate gay bars. He goes there occasionally in the evening, usually to meet friends. He is not sexually promiscuous, but occasionally will make a trip back to Boston. Down deep inside he would like to establish a meaningful interpersonal relationship, even find someone who could share his apartment with him; however, he is not only unsure about handling such a relationship but also is apprehensive about whether a close friendship with another male might raise certain suspicions about him. At this juncture in his life, he will count his blessings and just hope that nothing comes along to upset his "apple cart."

Maureen's story can be a shorter one. After finishing her degree in a state teacher's college she was fortunate to be given a contract to teach home economics in the high school in the same community. Since the college did have a master's program, she felt it wise after a year of teaching to start toward this goal on a part-time basis. It was during evening classes that she met Wilma, who was working with one of the social agencies in the community. They quickly became friends. This friendship developed into a love relationship. In order to be together and to reduce their expenses, they rented an apartment in which they lived for two years. An opportunity came to purchase a small house on the edge of town, so they financed a mortgage, and moved. Both enjoy working in the house and on the outside grounds. In five years they have made the place comfortable and attractive.

Neither Maureen nor Wilma are especially social. They have a few close friends. Each has a family they are concerned about. Family members raise no issue about their relationship; in fact, at holidays the two women are always together at one family home or the other.

Maureen is a responsible, hard-working, committed teacher. She seems appreciated by her students and will always respond to any extra duties the administration asks her to assume. Her lesbianism is no issue—certainly not as long as no one knows anything about it.

Are Gordon and Maureen a danger in the world of education? In a public gathering a former state commissioner of education rose to say that if he had ever known there were homosexual teachers in his school system, he would have had them discharged immediately. This would have been the end of Gordon and Maureen's careers if he had ever learned the truth about them. Should they be dismissed? This is a dilemma with which society is wrestling.

9

Peter – A Gay Clergyman

Dear Members of the Congregation,

Don't be frightened! You won't have to read this
letter; in fact, you will never see it. I am writing it at
the suggestion of my counselor. He had the feeling it
might help me in my next conference with him if I sat
down to put in writing some of the thoughts I might
have should I really be able to tell you all who I am.
He knows how distressed I become when I realize that
I have never been able to be totally honest with you.
You have known part of me. Over these past four years
many of you have been open with me and together we
have shared your joys and sorrows, your failures and
successes; but I have had to keep my real self shut off
from you; for this I feel deprived and hurt. However, I
am realistic; apparently it can be no other way and this
saddens me.

I hardly know where to begin. I guess I might just as
well say it right out—I am homosexual. There are
times I've wondered if some of you knew or at least
have been suspicious; if you have, you've been
considerate enough never to ask or even hint. I am
grateful for that. For the most part I don't think you
do know, since most people don't realize this about
me. I don't think I'm effeminate; I don't "swish," have
a high pitched voice, or have mannerisms which people
are apt to think identify one as gay. You know I enjoy
sports, was considered a good athlete at college, and
I've had a long interest in old cars—in fact, I'm pretty

good when it comes to tuning up an engine.

You may wonder how I managed to get ordained. You may suspect I lied; well, I didn't exactly, but I came close to it. Since the seminary faculty never seemed suspicious, the issue was never raised. The psychiatrist who examined me before I was finally approved never came right out and asked me the question. He did hint around about my sexuality, but I managed to skirt the issue. The Church board that examined me didn't ask and, although the district superintendent wondered about my plans for marriage, I was able to say "I don't think I'm quite ready. Probably some day." I was sure I would be hopelessly blocked if I told the truth.

I would not be honest if I did not say that I'm angry about this. If Christian ministers can't be honest, then who can? My own sense of right and wrong gets all mixed up. I presume I've been "political"; I don't like this but there seems to have been no other course. I felt called to the ministry, I think I have been and hope I will be a good "shepherd." I just had to adopt the old phrase "the end justifies the means," but I still don't like that kind of reasoning.

Frankly, what I've had to say to myself is: "Why can't a homosexual be a good pastor?" I have known and still know some other clergy who are gay. Some have served the Church with complete dedication for many years; even a full ministry. A few have made especially important contributions and served on important committees and commissions. They seem to have been highly respected in whatever situation they have had assigned; often they have been leaders in the broader community. I felt I could do the same. They must have had to hide, but they managed to cope without serious emotional stress to themselves, and they surely avoided any scandals which would destroy themselves or bring embarrassment to the Church.

I'm living in a world a little different from that of the gay clergy who have lived before me. This may be the reason I'm upset enough to feel I need to talk with someone—hence my sessions with a professional counselor. The last few years seem to have been bringing freedom to many who were once "imprisoned." The struggle for civil rights has been winning on so many fronts, and now gay people are finding courage "to get their act together." There is Gay Pride Week and the parades; gay organizations, even within some of the Churches; there is actually a "gay church," and recently I've heard of some gay synagogues. I would like to get involved; I think I should; but how can I? Even though I don't announce I'm gay, any association I have with this gay movement will create suspicions about me. If I were straight, then I'd be O.K. and could help; but being gay myself I just couldn't handle denying this if I were confronted.

I guess I'm angry. I'm angry because I have to be lonely. Oh, you might say: How can you say this? You have friends. You have all the people in this congregation who care about you. You get invited to dinners, to parties, to other social events. You are so busy, how can you be lonely? Well, I am! Lonely inside. I need to love someone, too. I want to be close —really close—to a few people who know me and accept me as I am. I wonder if you ever think about me in terms of my sexual frustrations. I've not taken any vows of celibacy. I'm still a young man and I have sexual drives. Usually, I'm totally frustrated. I don't want a sexual life with a woman; I just couldn't hack it. Although you will never see these words, I'm embarrassed to have to admit that it's only when I'm on some vacation far away that I can find some way of being sexual. But this, too, is frustrating. I can't follow through with a relationship. I can't let someone love me; I will hurt them too much, for I cannot imagine how I could make a meaningful commitment.

I don't know what the answer is to my situation. I don't expect you, or even my counselor to have one. I guess I may just have to muddle through like the other gay clergy before me. My only hope is that people like yourselves will grow more knowledgeable about homosexuality, that you will begin to see that homosexual persons, even those of us who are clergy or teachers, are not a threat to your children or to society as a whole. More than this, that you will develop some empathy about the hurt, the fear, the loneliness that lies deep within us and some day—oh, I hope it may come in my day!—let us know the joy of letting you know who we really are.

Yours in fellowship,
Peter McD.

Peter's name is legion. There is no possible way of knowing how many homosexual or bisexual clergy, seminarians, and other religious there are. Surely the number is far, far greater than is even suspected. In my counseling years I have worked with a significant number of men and women, who represent a whole list of denominational affiliations. I am confident other counselors can make the same kind of report. But we are only in contact with those who, like Peter, feel some need to talk about themselves with someone who can keep their confidence and can try to provide some support because of their feelings of frustration. There is no way of discovering how many are quietly, with stolid resignation, accepting their difficult situation and doing their best to convince those around them that they are straight or do not have any sexual conflicts whatsoever.

How incredible it is that people are apt to adopt the position that clergy and other religious are asexual. I wonder if they think that just because these persons have chosen—or, if you will, have been chosen for—such a vocation and may have been particularly blessed and set apart by the Holy Spirit that they cease being sexual. I recall a radio program during which Dr. Mary Calderone, director of SIECUS, made the comment to the effect that just because men and women were priests and nuns who took their particular vows of chastity and celibacy did not mean they ceased being sexual. Not long thereafter I had the privilege of sharing leadership of a conference of more than a hundred members of a women's religious order and I asked them if they felt Dr. Calderone's statement was a valid one. To a person, they responded in the affirmative. Father John McNeill, a Jesuit priest, who has lectured widely on human sexuality and especially about homosexuality, often makes the point that the way celibate clergy and religious really come to terms with their sexuality not only determines the joy that one can sense they feel but also it will color the way in which they relate to other persons. A helpful book on this subject is *The Sexual Celibate* by Donald Goergen.

Sex and sin have been closely associated in many minds. Perhaps it is deducted that since clergy are expected to sin little, they ought to have little sex. A few years ago I recall a young man telling about the wonderful minister he had when he was growing up, but he said he was always disturbed by the fact this pastor had children. It seemed somehow wrong that he must have engaged in sexual intercourse. Since there were only two children it was his hope that his minister's sexual experiences were limited to those two times when conception took place.

Slow progress, therefore, will be made as one attempts to deal with the subject of clergy and sex until it is realized that clergy and religious are total human beings, that God has created them out of the same clay as all men, and that they have similar sexual drives, needs, and frustrations as all God's children. Secondly, there must be a better understanding of and appreciation for sex, which over the past centuries has been dealt with as if it were the work of the devil rather than of a loving God.

On the point about the clergy being human, fully so, and also having similar sexual feelings to others of like sex, one has to look back to centuries of restriction, of discipline, and of denial. The argument is still heard that since Jesus did not marry, neither should those who are set apart as his special apostles or ambassadors. Jesus was a Jew; usually every Jewish boy was expected to marry and "be fruitful and multiply." If we believe that Jesus was truly human—this is creedal—then he was fully, totally man. It is heretical to believe he was half a man or that he was a divine person just using a human body. No, he was completely human and, therefore, as capable of knowing joy or experiencing pain as any other human being. No one can know what Jesus' sexuality may or may not have been, but how can it ever be said he was not sexual. He loved, he was close to persons. He was not an ascetic. He did have high regard for contract, for persons fulfilling commitments they made. Perhaps this is a reason why he did not marry. He no doubt had some insight that his life would be short. He may well have seen the cross ahead long before anyone else. How could he honestly marry, promise to be responsible for a wife and the children she might bear, if he could not fulfill this kind of obligation? Jesus surely says very little about sex. He does speak often about sin but this revolves around man's failure to love, to be good stewards, to serve God. He condemns hypocrisy, selfishness, those who "pass by on the other side," and those who refuse to forgive. Comments or instructions about sexual conduct do not seem to emanate from him.

Today many theologians point out the effect of stoicism and Hellenistic dualism upon the early Church. It is clear that Paul himself was affected by this prevailing thought. Even by the time many of the epistles were written, and surely during the period of the early Church, emphasis was laid upon the fact that the things of this world, even the human body itself, were potentially evil; only the spirit could be pure. It can therefore be deduced that since human sexuality is to be more identified with body than spirit, sex became something which was more to be tolerated than cherished; more to be deplored than exalted. This attitude, this position, has been indeed tenacious; it has marked the Church since the Christian hermits of the first centuries lived lives of asceticism, even neglecting their bodies to the point of never washing. This spirit, not always so extreme, marks the rise of monasticism and moves straight on into Protestant Puritanism. Even today there are pulpits still proclaiming that the desires of the body are evil. The formula survives: Sex equals sin.

With this background, it is no wonder that the man in the pew still has difficulty accepting the fact that the man at the altar is a whole man, that he is no different in what he is capable of feeling, and, more than this, that he probably has similar needs for love, for closeness, even for the expression of his sexual drives.

Thus, to understand that clergy are human, human as Jesus was, is of prime importance. If this can be accepted, then the second hurdle to clear is how can persons be helped to see that sex is good, not bad; that it is as God intended, not something with which man has been burdened; that it is creative, not merely procreative; and that through it man can find joy, wholeness, and fulfillment?

How damaging, how destructive, how corrupting has sex been throughout man's history? Has man's sexual needs created war? It may be true that Helen of Troy had the "face that launched a thousand ships," but could it be claimed that recent wars can be related to man's sexual drives? Today's prisons are overcrowded; how many inmates are there because of sexual crimes? Very few indeed. Convictions are primarily for robbery, fraud, sedition, conspiracy, manslaughter, murder—the list is long. The social history of man has dark moments: slavery, child labor, enforced poverty, the denial of education, corruption in high places. Can these be the result of man's sexuality?

Where do we find the root of sin? Are not Christians, at least, trying to say that we sin when we separate ourselves from God and from each other? Jesus has said: "Thou shalt love the Lord thy God with all thy heart and all thy mind, and thy neighbor as thyself." Again, he clearly stated: "I command that you love one another." If the Gospel has a single, solid message for the world it is found in this one word "love." This is what Jesus' ministry was all about; it was for this reason that he promised the Holy Spirit to all believers that they might be empowered to love.

Love has many enemies. Two of the greatest are money and power. Too often little attention is given to some familiar adages: "Money is the root of all evil." "Power tends to corrupt. Absolute power corrupts absolutely." Some careful thinking by all of us can help us see how some of the social ills already mentioned are the direct consequences of man's drive for money and power. It is ridiculous to say that these in themselves are totally bad. Money, since it is a rate of exchange, must exist. Even Jesus, upon reflecting on the Roman coin, responded with: "Render unto Caesar the things which are Caesar's." And he didn't totally condemn Zacceus because he was a rich man; he just helped him see the point of caring for others, of winning back some respect for himself by divesting himself of half of what he owned—he was allowed to keep the other half. It does seem, however, that Jesus did not want his own circle of the Twelve to be encumbered with money because he said they were to go on their journeys "without scrip." It was his hope that the workman would be worthy of his hire so that his men would have at least the necessities for survival. Power has to be recognized as a value in the sense that our social systems do have to have an established order, that there must be persons who are responsible agents to act with authority, provide judgments, and administer discipline. It is the abuse, not the use of power where the thin line always has to be drawn.

The point being made here, then, is that man's inhumanity to man has seldom been because of his sexuality. Man is still highly motivated by his strong drives for money and power. That they be won is not the problem; the moral issue is how does he attain them and how does he use them once he possesses them. It is in this arena that we need the theologians, the moralists, the teachers, the preachers. The evils of the sex drive seem minimal set against man's drive to win control over other men. It is time for the reordering of priorities.

Is it possible that the Church and society have been too preoccupied with man's sexuality? This may be an unfair statement, since it is only within the present century that reasonable, objective knowledge about human sexuality has become available. The truth about man's sexual nature has been revealed slowly. However, now that we do have facts provided through the disciplines of the natural as well as the social sciences, can we ignore them? Man has perhaps only been able to act upon what is "the known"; at the same time it has only been because man has not been satisfied with "the known" that progress and change have been possible. Man was not satisfied that the world was flat, that people of a certain skin color were intellectually inferior, that there is no cure for cancer, or that a man could never walk on the moon.

On the subject of human sexuality, new knowledge has been revealed about its physical aspects. Acceptance of such information has not been difficult. It is the insight about human sexual behavior, about sexual identities, and about sexual attitudes which cause consternation. Can we any longer categorically say that procreation is the primary purpose of sex? Is the only acceptable expression of sexuality to be within the contract of heterosexual marriage? Must the homosexual man or woman live a life without any genital expression of his or her sexuality? Is the transexual person thwarting the laws of nature and God's will if there is physical intervention to bring his sex and gender into harmony? Must the celibate who forgoes marriage, procreation, and specific genital acts be denied a sexuality which can be channeled through his love for and closeness to those who touch his life? These are the questions to which the Church and other social institutions must address themselves.

Because man has been misinformed about human sexuality, and because through this ignorance he has built his prejudices, his fears, and his censure, he has visited upon his fellow man an almost inconceivable inhumanity. Throughout the centuries men and women have suffered because they have not hewn to the narrow path of acceptable sexuality—they have been burned at the stake, imprisoned, banished, murdered in the gas chambers of Hitler's Germany, disinherited, discredited, denied forgiveness, and even thought not worthy of the name of Christian. Too often the Church, called to be the witness of God's love in the world, has either stood silent or even applauded.

We need to come back to Peter. What hope can we offer him? At this point of time, there is perhaps little to suggest. He may just have to continue to function as he presently does. It does appear that he is basically content about his Christian vocation. The members of his congregation are responding to his leadership. He has members who are kind to him so that he keeps socially occupied. His superiors apparently are not conscious of his homosexuality so that his future will not be blocked by his not having opportunities to work in areas beyond his local congregation. In fact, his chance for advancement will no doubt come in due time.

As much as he would like to challenge the system, one might be tempted to suggest he "play it cool." Although there would be many personal satisfactions if he could be involved in the gay movement, associate with those in a Gay Church organization or a Gay Church itself, such might not be politically wise. Many times he will be tempted to preach about homosexuality and unburden some of his feelings about society's mistreatment; but he will probably keep silent. Even to mention the fact in passing might give the hearers some clues he would not want them to pick up. He can give thought to having a program—perhaps a study group or series of workshops on human sexuality which would no doubt include consideration of homosexuality—but even this fairly mild approach might present certain risks. The best plan may be to say nothing, do nothing. This won't help his sense of frustration; but he has already learned that if he can't accommodate these frustrations, he won't be able to survive.

Asked to fantasize, what might Peter want if he could "rub Aladdin's lamp"? He might like to have everyone know that he is homosexual. This would save answering questions which constantly irritate him: Why doesn't he date? Why doesn't he plan to marry? Doesn't he want a family? Wouldn't a wife be a great asset to his ministry? No doubt he would like to believe his congregation would not go into some state of shock if they recognized that he did have sexual drives and needs which might even know moments of satisfaction. Ideally, of course, he might like to find someone of his own sex with whom he might develop a love relationship. This would be someone his congregation might know and respect as they would his own wife if he were married. He would then have someone with whom he could share intimately. They could be together often, they could attend social events, they could plan to enjoy holidays and summer vacations. It might just be great if this person actually shared the parsonage with him. Ideally there would be no objections from the congregation; only the basic response "Isn't it wonderful that Peter has someone with whom to share his life!" Sorry Peter; not now! When then? In another decade? Ever? Never? Who can say?

10

Craig – A Transvestite Husband

Dearest Sue,

I'm glad I left as early as I did this morning because that hard rain storm slowed up the driving. However, I did make my luncheon appointment on time. It was a good contact which may result in a fairly sizable order. It looks like a busy week out in this territory so I may not get home until late Friday night. At this point don't count on me for dinner. If plans change and I can break away earlier, I'll phone you on Thursday night.

This letter started off easily enough but suddenly it becomes difficult. The fact is, Sue, what I'm now trying to write has been written in my head a hundred different times. I've just never managed to get the courage to say what I guess I have to say. You may wonder why I've chosen this particular time to unburden myself. Well, I haven't told you, but I've seen a counselor three or four times about myself and my own particular problem. He has been helpful and now feels that I should make some effort to talk with you. I've wanted to do this, but for one reason or other the right moment doesn't come, or if it does, I seem to lose courage. A letter may be a coward's way out, but at this point it seems better to me.

I guess I'll ask you now to read, if you haven't already, the clipping I've enclosed which is a letter a wife wrote to Ann Landers. I cut it out a long time ago and have been wanting to share it with you. Again, the right moment never seemed to come. This isn't the only letter of its kind which Ann Landers has published, but it is one which particularly touched me because the wife seems understanding and also because Ann's comments are without any censure or condemnation. It has its humor, but it is also serious— to me at least.

Dear Ann Landers: Last May my husband asked me if he could wear one of my housedresses while painting the kitchen. He said it would be more comfortable. I said, "O.K." He did look awfully cute and I told him so. Ever since that time he has been wearing my dresses and wigs and makeup when we are alone. He has asked me to call him Linda when we "play girl friends," as he calls it.

I can truthfully say I don't mind. The only thing that bothers me is that he is prettier than I am. If we went out in public together he would get more whistles. Yesterday I read an article on sex deviation. It said men who enjoy dressing up in women's clothes are transvestites. I do not consider my husband abnormal. He is very manly in every way. He just happens to enjoy playing this little game. Is there anything wrong with it? I'd like your opinion.
　　　　　Happy Woman Who Loves Her Husband.

Dear Woman: My opinion is of no consequence. The only thing that matters is what you think, and apparently you think it is just fine. If you and your husband enjoy "playing girl friends," it's nobody's business. Just make sure the doors are locked and the shades down. And say hello to "Linda."

Yes, Sue, I am a transvestite. Does this shock you? My counselor says that you may know more than I think you know—most wives do—but since you've never made any comments, I can only believe that you know very little about my problem.

Of course I've been upset about this. Most of the time I feel so guilty; guilty that I didn't talk with you about it before we married, guilty that I haven't been able to share it during these ten years we've been together; guilty because it has stolen some of the little free time we have for ourselves; guilty because of the money I've spent and had to lie about. I guess it's this guilt plus the fact that I'm just tired of being so deceptive that I was forced to seek help.

I won't try at this point to go into details about what this counselor has been saying to me, but frankly I do seem relieved. He does think it will be helpful if we have a few more sessions. Also, since I've already given my O.K., he will be willing to talk with you alone or with both of us together. Perhaps this is a decision we can discuss over the coming weekend. Let's hope we can find some time together. Maybe you can get Beth to stay with the children Saturday night so that we could go out to dinner.

I apologize for "dumping on you" this way. I feel rotten about it. Still, I can only hope you will try to understand. I think our marriage is a good one. I love you very, very much; I always have. You must know this. I need you. Please believe me. Give Tim and Sharon a big hug for me.

Deepest love, always
Craig

T his letter is included here for two basic reasons: first, so that some distinctions can be made between the male homosexual who may "cross dress," i.e., wear clothing of the opposite sex, the transvestite, and the transexual; secondly, because the transvestite male, like the homosexual, is also in need of interpretation, understanding, and acceptance.

Our first task, then, may be to try and define terms. This is none too easy because in this arena clear-cut definitions are elusive. It is not a world of black and white; the gray predominates. It is possible to attempt some formal categorical statements which spell out determining differences, but having done so, one quickly thinks of persons who can't be fitted into some carefully devised formula. Therefore, any attempt at defining must be understood as being elastic. The majority of male homosexuals cannot be identified as being strongly feminine. Certainly it is to be recognized that in our present society, the words "masculine" and "feminine" are none too easy to pin down. Whole books reflecting serious study continue to be published on this subject. Having stated this, however, I am of the opinion that the majority of us who are part of what we term Western culture have a fairly good idea of what it means to be a boy or man or to be a girl or woman. It is probably safe to say that no one person is totally masculine or totally feminine. Again, there are the gray areas.

In years past, the clothes people wore provided a certain gender identity. This has now changed, but basically only in one direction. Females may now dress in clothes that were once identified as being for males and there is little social comment or criticism. Not long ago a well-established Main Street department store filled its display windows with female mannequins dressed in tailored suits, shirts, ties, heavy shoes and socks, felt hats, raincoats, and with accessories that are usually identified with men. Passersby didn't seem concerned about this. In fact, I'm sure that many considered it high style. I have always wondered what community reaction there might have been if the situation were reversed and there were male mannequins dressed as females. I suspect there would have been newspaper editorials; some denunciations from local pulpits and possibly street disturbances even ending in broken windows.

Back to definitions. "Drag" is a word often used in the homosexual world. It primarily refers to male homosexuals who will dress up in the clothing of the opposite sex. It needs to be made clear that the largest majority of male homosexuals don't want to cross dress, never have done so, and possibly never will. For some, doing so would almost be repulsive. On the other hand there are some male homosexuals, often very masculine, who on specific occasions do cross dress. There are drag parties held in homes or gay bars which, for the most part, are on traditional days such as Halloween; some will take this dressing seriously by trying to be as beautiful as possible and even want to pass in public; others will consider the dressing as being funny. Often at house parties, the host may get out an old trunk and guests will don various items. There may be miming of some of the movie stars and singers who are favorites with gay males: Mae West, Judy Garland, Bette Davis, Marlene Dietrich, Tallulah Bankhead, and others. This kind of activity is often referred to as "camp." For the most part it is innocuous fun. Those involved in the cross dressing are not taking it seriously. Ordinarily it can be said that the male homosexual is not basically interested in cross dressing; if such is done, it is usually in terms of masquerade or charade; he has no compulsion about it nor does it provide any sexual stimulation or excitement. That there are a few male homosexuals who take cross dressing more seriously than the majority is probably all too true, but it does bear repeating to say that the male homosexual primarily sees himself as a male, he wants to be known as a male, he likes his male genitalia, he enjoys male orgasm, and he is primarily or even exclusively interested in having another male as his sex partner or lover.

The transexual person will be discussed in a following chapter, but for the sake of some clarification it is important at this point to draw the basic distinction between the transvestite and the transexual. In the serious evaluation of transexualism it becomes necessary to separate the words "sex" and "gender." When a child is born, the attending physician is expected to provide a sex identification. He says "This baby is a boy" or "this baby is a girl." Usually his task is not difficult. Practically from the moment of birth, the family and friends begin to relate to this child as one sex or the other. As this boy or girl begins to grow, all who are related or concerned in one way or the other will be directive and supportive to help these individuals to a matching gender identity which is masculine for boys, feminine for girls. This program generally works well; however, and for reasons excessively difficult to determine, there are instances when it just doesn't. The result is an individual with one sex identity and an opposite gender definition. The majority of professionals who have labored to understand transexualism over the past two decades are of the opinion that this identity is established in the early years of life and that attempts to reverse it in the mature years when it is diagnosed are unsuccessful. Spelled out in all too simple terms it is said that the transexual person is one who is caught, imprisoned in the wrong body. In other words, a male may look as if he is a man, but for all intents and purposes he is in reality a woman; a female may have every outward appearance of being a woman, but in truth she is a man. This transexual person, possibly well before ever receiving professional help, may cross dress but in doing so is actually only trying to be the person he or she is. In this instance we are not dealing with homosexuality nor with transvestism as it is being explained in this chapter.

We need to return to Craig. He was born into what might be called an average middle-class American family. Both parents had a high school education. Father was a veteran of the Second World War and married as soon as he enlisted. Since he never did overseas duty, he and his wife were often able to live together near the base where he was stationed. Craig and his older sister were born during that period; two younger children were born after the war when the family had settled in a midwestern community where the father obtained a civil service job. There is nothing particularly unusual about Craig's family life or his early development. The parents were Church-oriented and seemed to have a good relationship. The children were involved in the usual community organizations; all of them seemed generally bright and related well to their peers. Craig maintains he considers himself fortunate in having had the family background he has had. He is grateful to his parents and is proud of his sister and brothers.

During junior high, Craig was active in scouting and enjoyed summer camp experiences. He learned to swim during these summers and when he began high school he pursued swimming as his major sport, eventually becoming a team star. As a teen-ager he fit the traditional pattern. He joined two or three high school clubs, worked at a local store two or three afternoons a week to help support the ten-year-old car he had, dated various girls, and usually was involved with school and community social events.

It was at college, his sophomore year, that he met Sue. They began dating quite seriously in their junior year and were married the month of their graduation. Sue's background was little different from his except that her father, a fairly successful businessman, had died while she was in high school and her mother, who had been trained as a teacher, had taken a teaching post to help with her college education and that of her brother.

Craig found a sales job with a growing company soon after he graduated from college and although he had to move to the east, this was not a serious problem to either him or Sue. The two children arrived in the first five years of marriage. They have not wanted more children. Sue has been primarily a homemaker except that she does some volunteer community and church work from time to time. Craig, because his sales position keeps him away from home during the greater part of each week, cannot be too involved with the community although he is active in their church.

Craig's transvestism has a certain classic pattern. As a young child, since his sister was only a year and half older, he recalls how the two of them used to play house. They would reverse roles and he would dress as the mother and wear some of his sister's clothes. He remembers that once, with other playmates, they held a wedding. It was great fun that he could be the bride with some lace curtains from the attic. When he was seven or eight, such open demonstrations ceased because he began to feel self-conscious and didn't want to be teased. He started to masturbate when he was around twelve or thirteen. He always felt guilty. He did get especially "turned on" about female clothes. There were a few times, when his younger brother with whom he shared his bedroom, might be sleeping at a buddy's house, that he slipped out in the night and took his sister's bathing suit off the line and put it on. He would lie on his bed and feel excited. Sometimes he masturbated. Getting the bathing suit back on the line again and then sneaking back to his room gave him the feeling that he'd accomplished his mission. The secrecy, even the element of daring, was stimulating. Occasionally, when the right situation offered itself, he would borrow his sister or mother's clothes, dress up, walk around his room, admire himself in the mirror, and then carefully replace the clothes in the hope that he would not be discovered. He felt all this was somehow wrong, but there was some inner compulsion which he just could not control. Often after such a cross dressing experience, he would vow not to do it again—but he did.

As he matured into the teen years, his sexual interests involved girls. There had been a few cursory homosexual experiences, but they were not satisfying. He felt "dirty" about them. During high school, he dated several girls and got serious with a couple of them. There was the usual necking and petting, but with the fairly strong value system provided through scouting, Church, and his swim coach he didn't engage in actual sexual intercourse. His cross dressing in the later high school years and early college days was minimal. He thought about it but struggled to avoid succumbing to the urge.

In college, after he and Sue began to move into a deeper relationship, his sexual needs were high, and when they seemed to have some agreement about marriage they began a sexual relationship which was not too frequent because of separated dorms and strict college regulations.

It was not long after the marriage that the drive to cross dress became strong and at times overwhelming. Because his wife was small her clothes were not practical; also there was too much fear that she would suspect. He was too self-conscious about buying feminine clothing in any local stores, but since he traveled, he felt comfortable, considering he was a married man, of buying items "for his wife"—as he told the sales clerks. Also, he took a post office box and began ordering from mail-order catalogues articles that he hesitated to purchase personally in a store. Since he was a salesman and had business suitcases which he always kept locked, he kept these clothes in the suitcases and locked in the trunk of his car.

His cross dressing took place away from home. He preferred motels over hotels when he traveled. This way it was easier to carry his cases from car to room without suspicion, and there was less chance of being interrupted by maids or other hotel personnel. At first he only dressed in his room and admired himself in the mirrors. He was actually convincing in his female role. Having been a swimmer he did not have highly defined muscular arms; he possessed a sensitive face, had good color and unblemished skin. His body structure was not heavy. He had kept his weight down. His body hair was light in color; in fact, the little he did possess had not appeared until his twenties. His legs were quite shapely; his feet not large.

As the incidences of his cross dressing increased and he worked toward as much perfection as possible, he became more confident that he might be able to venture out without being discovered. The first time was traumatic. He just went from his motel room to his car parked near the building and drove around that particular neighborhood for about ten minutes. All kinds of fear overtook him. What if he had a flat tire? Suppose he had an accident and had to produce his license? What would happen if he were injured in an accident and taken to the hospital? When he got back safely to his motel room he felt emotionally exhausted. He resolved not to do that again. But, of course, he did. In fact, he grew braver and braver so that soon he was driving into downtown business streets and even taking short walks. Eventually he went to a movie, and finally got the courage to go to a small, quiet restaurant for dinner. Fortunately his voice was on the tenor side and he had practiced speaking as softly as possible. In ordering his meal, he spoke as few words as possible. The waiter had wanted to be friendly, but Craig, while trying to be pleasant, discouraged conversation.

Every now and again, Craig became conscious of how ridiculous his life had become. He realized his was not some unique, isolated problem; he knew there were other transvestites. He also heard there were some organizations. He was tempted to make contact with them but was too apprehensive. This behavior began to take away time from his work responsibilities. There were occasions when he might have returned home to be with the family rather than staying an extra night on the road to play his game. Also money was involved: wigs, clothes, shoes, cosmetics, accessories. He was trying to hide them as part of his traveling expenses, but Sue was beginning to question higher professional costs and a reduction in the cash available for home and family.

One day he made a decision he had pondered for a long time. He would stop this charade. He did. While in a city he often visited, he packed up all his feminine clothes and just dropped them off at the local Salvation Army which maintained a storeroom of second-hand clothes and furniture. The cosmetics and a few items went into an incinerator. That was the end of that! Until three months later. Then it started all over again.

It was two years after this that he knew he needed help. In addition to the problems, now even more serious, which brought about the decision to give away his feminine clothes the first time, there were two traumatic events, quite close together, which shook him badly. Since his first venturing out to a movie and to dinner, he had gotten even braver. He had occasionally gone into a cocktail lounge or bar frequented by heterosexuals. Craig was not a heavy drinker, in fact he used alcohol sparingly. He was not trying to get involved with anyone. It was just the excitement of being in such an environment where he might pass as a woman and even be admired by men who might be there. The first trauma occurred when a man, alone at the bar and a bit inebriated, came and sat at the table bringing along a drink. He was eager to start a conversation; it was also obvious he was interested in picking up someone. Craig kept a certain composure, talked as little as possible, and parried any of the suggestive overtures the man made. Finally, sensing he was being rejected, the man, surely not very sober, said "What's the trouble? What's wrong with me? Are you some kind of a queer?" With that Craig quickly pushed away from the table and fled toward the parked car.

The second episode also followed an evening at a lounge when he had stayed too long and consumed more alcohol than he could handle. Driving back to the motel, he went through a stop sign at an intersection which was often watched by a police cruiser. He was soon stopped and his license demanded. This was a moment he hoped would never happen. The officer looked at the name then looked at Craig. He also sensed that Craig had been overdrinking. He asked Craig where he was staying. The motel was nearby. The policeman was both sensitive and generous. First he quietly tried to have Craig understand the seriousness of the situation and explain what heavy consequences might be involved. He warned him that he ought to get help. At that point he said he would follow him to the motel. There was no ticket, no arrest, but there was the firm statement from the officer that he hoped they would not meet again in a similar situation.

Craig had been lucky. He knew it. He must do something. No longer could he continue to risk so much of his future—his marriage, his home, his job, his reputation in church and community. As soon as he was back home, he went to a pay phone and contacted the Help Line in the largest city in the state, only forty miles from his own community. He could be anonymous. He was given the name of a professional counselor who would see him without his having to reveal his name or employment situation. He followed through. The sessions which took place relieved much of his tension and anxiety. It was eventually through this that he had the courage to write his letter to Sue.

What could a counselor do for him? First there had to be an open, honest relating of his life: his early years, his family relationships, his sexual feeling and fantasies, his interpersonal contacts with persons of both sexes and whatever genital sexual encounters there may have been, his marriage to Sue, his feelings toward his children. The experienced counselor could see a traditional pattern: a heterosexual male in a comfortable marriage yet having to deal with the compulsion to cross dress. His life-style away from home had grown too bizarre. It was creating great anxiety and tension within him, his guilt feelings were not being resolved, he was plagued about not being able to share his total self with Sue. These and the risks already mentioned were all too real.

It was possible for the counselor to help him understand himself better, to realize that his transvestism was not as uncommon as he thought, to know that he was not emotionally ill, to help him believe that he did not have to be so guilt-ridden; and then, with the counselor, to consider some way to cope more satisfactorily with his problem.

The wife very often either has definite knowledge or well-developed suspicions of a husband's cross dressing long before he imagines she does. Most often she will say little or nothing. She just waits until the husband either does something that brings the situation into the open or is willing to finally unburden himself to her. If the marriage is a good one and there has been fairly solid communication on all other levels, then there is usually an understanding response from the wife. No doubt this is a matter with which she would rather not deal, but it usually isn't difficult to project that other situations might be far more traumatic: a serious relationship with another woman, a homosexual identity, some distressing physical illness, or some scandal which might bring trauma to the total well-being of the family.

If they should come together to the counselor, then it could be determined what outside help might be useful. From a therapeutic point of view, totally dispelling the compulsion, the drive to cross dress is all too challenging. Few therapists would want to undertake this as a counseling goal. If his wife can be understanding about his problem, if they can talk about it together, if they can arrive at some conclusion how he can cross dress (if this continues to be his need) without it becoming a public matter, and if there can be a counseling situation comfortable for both of them when they sense such need, then they might manage to handle their future with the kind of honesty and sharing they had not even known previously.

One other practical help often available to the transvestite is contact with other transvestites. There are some reputable organizations which make this possible through letters, exchanging of pictures, and even actual meetings. Also, at least in larger cities, there are groups of transvestites which meet either regularly or for special occasions. Such groups keep rather secretive, as might be expected, but they do often make themselves known to professional persons so that referrals can be made to them.

Before leaving the story of Craig, I want to make a few comments about transvestism which, in part at least, find substance in his life situation. It is my contention that of all those identified as being a sexual minority, the transvestite may experience an unusual amount of emotional pain and anxiety. Obviously his greatest difficulty centers around the need for secrecy. As has already been mentioned, our Western society has little difficulty about a female dressed in male attire, but the male who dons female clothing is not only open to ridicule but also may be in trouble with the law or even risk bodily harm. No doubt many interesting comments could be postulated about this negativism which, in my mind, centers around masculinity fears, but such a discussion would be a long one. The sheer reality is that by far the majority of men, and indeed many women too, cannot emotionally cope with a man such as Craig dressed as a female. It is true they can watch a female impersonation, may even attend a "drag show" or laugh at a comedian who is intending to be humorous in his cross dressing; but accepting the Craigs is all too challenging.

Provided a man is not cross dressing to defraud or to adopt the female role for some reason which helps him fulfill a criminal purpose, I can find no reason for determining that transvestism is ethically immoral. I will have to take the position that Craig is a basically moral man. He has kept his marriage vows, he loves his wife and children, he earns his living, he is Church-oriented, he tries to help in community affairs, and, all in all, he seems to have a solid value system. It is true that his cross dressing is using money which might be better spent and that he also, because of this need, is spending more time away from the family than he should. Beyond this, I find it difficult to fault him.

Finally, I am trying to indicate that the transvestite, perhaps of all the so-called sexual minorities, may know the most rejection while at the same time he is doing little or no harm to any other persons. He often lives a lonely life within himself; he can experience real fear; he is open to harassment and ridicule; and, unless his loved ones can understand and accept him, he may know serious emotional pain and rejection. It may help if he finds other transvestites with whom he can share. It can also help if, like Craig, he finds a counselor whom he can trust. But above all it will be the love, the concern, and the empathy which is exhibited by his family and friends which will be his greatest support.

11

Keith – A Transexual Son

Dear Mom and Dad,

This is the second attempt at writing you a letter, and I am not sure whether it will ever get completed and mailed. Actually, what I have to tell you is something I've been thinking about for quite a while and living with even longer. Yet I hesitate to share this since nothing final has been decided; and it seems pointless to alarm you unnecessarily.

Now that you plan to visit me this summer, I feel that perhaps you should know in advance what you may find when you get here. You may not want to make the trip if you find what I am about to tell you unacceptable. At some point you must find out anyway, and I have debated with myself when that should be. I've decided, at least for today, that maybe it would be best to hear it by letter rather than have you come here and gradually discover that I have been hiding something from you.

You ask, "What have you been hiding?" Well, actually, I have been hiding it not only from you but from myself in the sense that I could not face up to who I am and then decide what I was going to do about it.

After Laura decided that she did not want to live with me this past fall, I knew that there was no longer any point in running from myself. I went to see one of those expensive Park Avenue psychiatrists who is quite familiar with my kind of problem. After an hour's

interview he referred me to a clinic which works with
people like myself. His diagnosis of my condition
confirmed what I thought but was afraid to face. His
tentative judgment is that I am a transexual person.
Such a person, while physically normal sexually,
nevertheless thinks, feels, and desires to be of the
opposite sex and gender. People like myself are not
homosexuals. These are content with their gender and
do not wish to change, but are attracted to people of
the same sex. I repeat: I am not a homosexual, but
rather a person who experiences himself as being more
feminine than masculine. I know that must boggle the
mind. Me—big, tall, deep voiced, and craggy—thinking
of myself as being a woman! But if you consider it
weird looking at me from the outside, just imagine how
confusing it is to be the one on the inside looking out.
I am forever breaking up in laughter or breaking down
in tears when I see how hopeless it is.

By now you are probably wondering if I am drunk or
high on pot or flipped out over the loss of the
marriage and the kids. I assure you none of these is
the case. If you will think back, I am sure you will
remember the time you found out that I cross dressed.
Actually, from the time of puberty none of my sexual
fantasies were "right" in that I never wanted to take
the active and aggressive role, but instead imagined
myself as being the female partner.

I never would have married Laura had she not taken
an aggressive interest in me sexually prior to marriage.
Afterward, she became exceedingly passive and
indifferent; in the face of such unresponsiveness I
found it difficult to achieve any kind of sexual release.
Our problems, as far as she was concerned, however,
were "more money" rather than "more sex." In one
sense that reflects something of my nature in that I was
not aggressive enough and success-oriented like the
average male. The point I'm trying to make, is that my
gender problem predated the marriage. I hung onto
the marriage out of love for the children and the blind
hope that it could save me from myself. That is too

much to ask of a marriage, even a good one, which ours never was.

Well, you are probably wondering what am I going to do about myself. For one thing, I am not going to repeat the mistake of thinking marriage will cure me. It won't. Neither will expensive psychiatrists, who for the most part have admitted defeat in trying to change the gender orientation of transexuals. We are too poorly motivated for them to help us. For in every respect except gender we are well-adjusted, normal people. We do not wish to change our identity any more than you do. It's not our personalities we wish to alter but our bodies; psychiatrists can do little to help in that department. Many of my transexual friends have spent small fortunes on psychiatrists; however, no one definitely knows what causes nor can cure "gender dysphoria" (the technical term).

At this point you may be asking yourselves: What did we do wrong? Believe me, you did your best. Transexuals come from all kinds of family situations. There don't seem to be any characteristics that these families share which would account for this condition. Consequently, the experts think it must be a combination of factors: genetics, early environment, or possibly some prenatal condition. Whatever its causes, perhaps only God knows. How many times I've looked at myself in the mirror in the morning and asked why? But it doesn't make the slightest difference, even if I did know the answer, because I still have to live this way, at odds with myself, stuck with a body that doesn't fit the person within.

By now you must be convinced that I am playing with half a deck, that I am a candidate for the nearest nut house. You are right, of course. It might seem as if anyone who feels as I do has obviously slipped a cog somewhere along the line and ought to be watched carefully so that children aren't molested or national secrets betrayed to the Russians. For years I lived with immense guilt over being so weird. But one thing the visit to the psychiatrist and the clinic did do, along

with meeting other transexuals, has been to help me
get over the guilt that has made me so insecure and
unsure of myself. I know who I am; now no matter
what anyone else may say or think about it, I am not
ashamed of being me anymore. That, in itself, has
helped me greatly in relating to people even as a
teacher. Before, I could not help always feeling a little
insecure, a little defensive, lest I betray myself or give
away some clue as to my real identity. I always had to
attempt to prove my worth, be it intellectually or some
other way. Well, I suppose I still do that at times, but
now I am not driven to do it.

In short, one of the benefits of coming out of the
closet, as they say, is that one can be more honest and
open with people. It is a good feeling, believe me.
Imagine yourself cooped up for the past twenty-five
years always fearful that someone will discover the
awful truth that will destroy you as a person. Then one
day you realize that either you come out voluntarily or
your compulsions will drive you out accidentally.
Because of fear of the latter happening, I chose to seek
help and come out on my own. That experience was
like being born again.

Of course, I have not made a public announcement
of all this to the community or to my old friends. But
they surely noticed the change in me and liked it, even
though they probably are a bit perplexed by my long
hair and bracelets.

What of the kids? They don't know either, at least
overtly, even though there have been a few incidents
that have surely raised questions in their minds. Yet
they still love me in spite of my peculiarities. I have
not wanted to shock them with the news until I must.
By then I hope they will be older and more able to
understand. This is why, incidentally, that I have been
willing to let the children return to Laura. It will be
easier for them later, and easier for me now in not
having to keep it from them all the time.

I speak of later. At some point in the future, possibly
two or three years hence, there may come a time of

major decision-making for me. Right now I am feeling my way along and learning more about who I really am. In addition, there is much to learn besides how I feel. While some transexuals make the change very successfully, eventually remarrying or taking responsible positions in society, passing from one sex role to another requires an immense amount of self-discipline and training over a period of years. Along the way people have dropped out, changed their minds, or given up and taken the easy way out— suicide. That grim alternative indicates why this is not really a cute idea that someone gets in his head. It is something we must do no matter what cost, suffering, or time may be involved. When it seems utterly hopeless (and depression is our biggest problem) some give up on life altogether.

For the present, I try to live one day at a time, being patient with the progress I'm making. I should tell you that I am seeing a physician who has prescribed hormone therapy for me. This has a calming effect on me and with continued use brings about a modest feminization of the body. In addition, I am receiving electrolysis to remove my beard. Also I am regularly participating in a support group of transexual persons. I tell you of the treatment I am receiving to indicate to you that I am serious about what I am doing. The final decision, however, is well out in the future. Obviously, surgery is the last and irreversible step. Before that happens both the doctors and I want to be sure that this is right for me so that I can function in the gender role of my choice.

There is much for me to do before making the last big decision. I want to check the openings for me in various other fields of work. If possible I would like to get some training that I could use later on, maybe in the field of speech therapy, since I myself will need to spend considerable time learning to modify my voice.

Anyway, I need time to work things out, so don't be in a panic that you are about to "lose a son." I am reminded of that old cliché about parents whose son marries, "Don't worry, you're not losing a son, you're just gaining a daughter." In my case, how much more appropriate!

I'm sorry if my humor shocks you. You see, I've had to learn that the choice is either to laugh over this or to cry. Humor keeps me going, and weeping just leaves me exhausted and depressed. Like me, perhaps it is best that you take this one step at a time. Who knows what will happen? Perhaps something will occur to make me content the way I am at present, or even to remarry as a man. (If I stop the hormone treatment, I am told the masculine characteristics may return.) Nothing final has happened—yet.

I thought it best to tell you. I hope this is the right decision. I could have waited much longer, until I was ready for surgery and absolutely sure, thus no doubt saving you a lot of worry. But then it would have come as an even greater shock and surprise for which you would have had little time to make an adjustment. This way you will have more time to talk to me about it and understand how I feel. I certainly don't want to cause you hurt or embarrassment. Maybe this way will give you time to gradually accept this situation before I have gone too far for you to catch up. I hope this is the right way to tell you. I've suffered enough over this not to want to cause others great pain, yet I know it won't be easy for anyone.

I want you to know that I love you both very much. You have not failed me in any way, but have given much more of yourselves than I could ever repay. I have often thought that if I could just wait until you were no longer living, I would be sparing you this anxiety. So help me, I can't write this without breaking down—Mom and Dad, I can't wait! I can't fight it any longer! Please believe me, if there were any other way to keep from hurting you and my kids I would do it.

As things are, it's been all I could do to keep functioning all these years. The fact that I must continue to live in a male role for the immediate future is bearable because I feel as if I am making some progress toward an eventual change. Were that not possible, I don't know how I could go on. I just hope you can understand. I can't say much more because my feelings are getting out of hand.

I don't know when I will mail this. Maybe later, maybe never, so don't be surprised if you get it months after the date on it. I'll let it sit on my desk awhile and see if I still feel like sending it. The first letter didn't make it for just that reason so maybe this one won't either. Yet in some ways I think it is easier to tell you this way rather than wait until you are here and have me beating around the bush or blurting it out at the dinner table.

As I get ready to close this letter I am mindful of the confusion you face as to what name you should use. My friends who know, call me Kim, but I don't expect you to do that. Call me your son or whatever you are comfortable with. I'm still me whatever you call me.

My love to you both,
Keith

Keith's letter is a long one but it does spell out clearly some of the pain and anxiety which transexual persons bear. During the past twenty-five years, ever since the emergence of Christine Jorgensen, which was marked by a certain sensationalism, the public has been exposed to other transexual persons who have caught the interest and attention of the media; such as Jan Morris, who as John went as the reporter on Hillary's successful ascent of Mt. Everest and who later authored *Conundrum* to tell her story, and Renee Richards, successful physician and champion tennis player. It would seem as if a certain glamor surrounds such prominent persons with the result that the agony which all transexuals know as they move through the process of sex change may be all too minimized.

Transexual persons have lived in every century and been within every culture; however, it has only been within the last two or three decades that this phenomenon has been identified and is now recognized by many professions representing a variety of disciplines. It was Dr. Harry Benjamin of New York who, as an endocrinologist, began to reach out and provide medical help and support to those whom he, with others, were to diagnose as transexual. His writings, his expertise, and his compassion soon attracted the interest and support of other responsible professionals to the extent that Johns Hopkins Hospital in Baltimore was willing to establish the first clinic in the United States. Since then other clinics have been established throughout the country. For nearly a decade an international symposium on gender identity has been held every other year, attracting representatives, particularly from the fields of sociology, psychology, and medicine so that new experiences and new knowledge might be shared. Over many years, the Erickson Educational Foundation of Baton Rouge and New York has provided generous support to educational and research projects. This pioneer foundation brought its work to an end during 1977; however, many aspects of the foundation's purposes are to be continued through the Janus Information Facility of the University of Texas Medical Branch, Galveston, Texas. Mrs. Zelda Suplee, long associated with the Erickson Foundation, will continue to share her extensive knowledge of this subject in her new role with the recently established facility in Galveston.

Although many transexual persons are seeking out individual doctors and other specialists to help them in terms of evaluation, emotional support, hormonal therapy, and surgery, there is a growing consensus that it is the well-established and responsible clinic which may be the wisest approach. At this point there are several such clinics scattered throughout the United States. They all have their distinctive marks and have established their own methods of procedure. It may be informative to describe the one clinic which I know well as a board member. It is formally chartered and incorporated as the Gender Identity Clinic of New England and functions in Hartford, Connecticut. Its president, the head of the Department of Obstetrics and Gynecology of a local hospital, had a ten-year relationship with a large, prominent hospital which pioneered in the area of transexualism. There are two psychiatrists, a clinical psychologist, a lawyer, a nurse, two plastic surgeons, an endocrinologist, a social worker, and specialists in other helping fields. Any candidate for the clinic can be referred by any of the team members or by other social agencies. However, before being presented to the board, the candidate must be seen personally and evaluated by the president of the clinic, the two psychiatrists, and the clinical psychologist. It may be that others of the board will also have interviewed the candidate. When all the reports are completed, the candidate is invited to appear before the board. Each board member is free to ask questions; and each candidate may use this opportunity to clarify doubts or concerns. After the candidate has been seen, the board must determine some course of action. Any positive decision to identify and accept a candidate as a transexual who may eventually move onto surgery must be unanimous. If there are doubts about identity, then there is the recommendation of further evaluation, continued psychotherapy, and an imposed waiting period.

When there is the positive decision to accept a person for hormonal therapy the males-to-females are scheduled for estrogen, and the females-to-males are given testosterone. The basic clinic rules call for a person living cross dressed in the intended gender role for at least one year before surgery. No final procedures are performed unless those who are married have received a formal divorce. Persons are not accepted by the clinic if there is a criminal record, nor if there is evidence of serious emotional or psychological impairment.

When the prescribed time period has elapsed and when all of the clinic requirements have been fulfilled, the candidate appears before the board for the final decision about surgery. When the time for surgery comes, in the case of the male-to-female transexual, the male genitalia are removed and a vagina is created; for the female-to-male transexual there is breast surgery and a hysterectomy (some penis construction is taking place but this is still a field of experimentation).

Too often in the past, follow-up of patients has not been

careful enough; however, the New England Clinic is keeping contact with postoperative patients through medical check-ups, by making board members available for continuing help, and by expressing concern for a patient's socialization process.

An adjunct to this clinic has been a social grouping known as the XX Club (XX meaning "trans-sex"). This group pre-dates the clinic since it first was brought into being to provide an opportunity for individual transexuals to share their feel-ings, their fears, and their concerns. It was also a situation in which those questioning their gender identity could discuss themselves with those who did feel secure. Over the years many who may have thought they were transexual came to realize such was not the fact. This group, now democratically organized, is also concerned about their own education, about providing accurate information for the public, and working toward the legal and civil rights of all who make up our sexual minorities. Group members have developed deep concerns about each other so that they serve as a major support to those undergoing surgery and for the period which follows.

Keith's letter pinpoints many of the difficult problems which must be faced by those who come to the realization they are transexual and who eventually set sex reassignment as their goal. Obviously each individual has particular or even unusual hurdles with which to cope, but there are certain difficulties which almost every transexual must wrestle with once even a tentative decision is made about proceeding. All too briefly I will try to highlight a few of them.

Identity. Establishing the true and definitive fact that an individual is gender dysphoric may be a complicated process. Of course it varies from individual to individual. Professionals in this field are generally convinced that the roots of such an identity reach back into early childhood. There seems little evidence to support the position that there is any genetic de-termination or an endocrine imbalance. It is rare to find any chromosome abnormality. It becomes clearer that the basic problem lies in the early psychosexual development of the individual. To attempt to pinpoint specifics is almost impossible. One has to depend upon how a person feels, how he or she conceives the self, and how far back these feelings are remembered. Generally, as childhood experiences and feelings are reported, there is the response "I felt like a girl." or "I felt like a boy." Those on the outside who attempt to reach a conclusion about this identity, must rely on the information the individual provides. Obviously some situations are more clear-cut than others and there are certain traditional patterns. Physical appearance, mannerisms, and voice placement may provide some clues, but they are not definitive by any means. In the final analysis, the individual ends up having to make his or her decision about the self; assisting professionals are at hand to evaluate, to support, and finally to affirm if such consent falls within their own consciences. This identity is not necessarily a laborious one in every situation, but for many it is long and often tortuous.

The Family. This seems an unavoidable area of anxiety and pain. Since the majority of transexuals who are giving consideration to sex reassignment are probably between twenty and thirty-five, one or both parents will usually be living. Generally speaking, persons do not want to hurt parents or upset them unduly, especially if the parents are in the middle and later years. So often a counselee will say "But if only my parents didn't ever have to know!"

The reaction expressed by parents will vary greatly. My experience indicates that none receive the news with joy. There is often bewilderment, guilt, anger, apprehension, fear, and denial. Moving parents through these negative attitudes and into a positive, supportive frame of mind is slow, painful, and challenging. From time to time the resistence will be high and determined almost all the way through. It may not be until after sex reassignment that parents begin to relate to the new identity of their son or daughter so that acceptance takes place. On the positive side it can be reported that parents have said,"We had such a poor relationship with John, but now we are so happy with Joan."

Parents are not the only family members to think about.

There are brothers and sisters, grandparents, aunts, uncles, and others. Occasionally the greatest resistance will come from family members other than the parents. It is also a fact that now and again the major support will come through a brother or aunt or some person in the family with whom the transexual may have a particularly close, understanding relationship.

As in the case of Keith, many transexuals, both male and female, may be married and have children. This provides a whole new arena of difficulty. The responses a spouse may make to the realization that a partner is transexual run the gamut from early and comfortable acceptance to outright angry, unbending rejection. On the other hand, some have relationships they do not wish to break even when surgery takes place; others may want to remain as friends, while there are those who insist on final separation with a complete cutoff of communication. When there are children involved the problem is more confounded. Obviously the attitude of the spouse will determine how much or how little the transexual person will continue to relate to children. Obviously there are many variables here: the age of the children, their own emotional strength, the feelings they may or may not have had about the parent who has withdrawn from the home. It is here that the transexual person often needs counseling help.

Vocation: Transexual persons seem to appear in every vocation. They are in all the professions, work in offices, are sales people, and even operate steam shovels. From an ideal point of view it might be best if the majority could remain in their chosen vocation and even keep the jobs they have held for a long period. There are isolated instances where the latter is and has been possible; however, for the majority this is not true. If, as some clinics insist, a person must live cross dressed in the desired gender role for a year, then this work shift will generally have to take place before the eventual surgery. It is not too conceivable to expect an employer to permit an employee to leave work on Friday night as "Sam" and report on Monday morning as

"Sally." The social dynamics of the situation are too traumatic.

In many instances, therefore, either movement to another similar work situation, removal to a new community, or even a change of vocation is necessary. This, of course, is not impossible so that the majority of those undergoing sex change manage to survive. Unfortunately there are instances in which this kind of wrenching eventually seems impossible and the transexual will come to the eventual decision either to forego, or at least to postpone for a long period of time, any final effort to live cross dressed or to undergo surgery.

Finances: There are few situations in which dollars and cents, or the lack of such resources, do not cause grave concern. I am sure that every clinic and individual physicians and surgeons can attest to the fact that there are long lists of identified transexuals who want and need sex reassignment but who cannot meet the costs. Fees vary, but since there are hospital expenses and professional fees, the "bottom line" is in thousands of dollars. At this point, help through governmental agencies is nonexistent. Some hospital plans and a few insurance companies will underwrite major expenses. Those in any welfare situation seem without any help whatsoever. For the majority the specter of inadequate financial resources is ever constant.

Beyond finding the actual needed cash for sex reassignment itself, there are the problems of day-to-day living expenses, the loss or reduction of earning power which comes in the shifting of work situations, and, for the previously married person, the ongoing responsibilities of child support and possible alimony. There are no ready answers to this complicated problem. Each situation must be dealt with on its own.

Physical Appearance: Primarily this affects the male-to-female transexual. Obviously it is a happier state when the person has evident feminine characteristics. This is not always true. Many males have strong, dominant masculine characteristics; heavy beards, receding hair lines, large structures, and deep voices. Beards are always a difficult challenge. Electrolysis is needed; the process is long, tedious, and costly. Hair styling and/or wigs are essential. Proper wardrobes and how they are used become a priority. There may have to be instruction in the whole feminization process. Although hormones are helpful in lowering the voice of the female-to-male transexual, the male-to-female acquires little change in pitch through this medical assistance. It may be that only sustained voice training will be able to help.

Legal: There are many legal procedures which plague the transexual. Some are easier than others. It is not difficult to procure a legal name change, to alter Social Security identification, and in most instances to change Church records, school and professional records, and accounts in banks and stores. In some states it may be complicated to receive a new driver's license; in the majority of states it is still impossible to have a new birth certificate issued. Professional legal advice is important when it comes to the question of trusts, possible inheritances, the making of wills, and the joint ownership of properties, real or otherwise. It is apparent, then, that although the majority of legal procedures are possible, they often provide their own irritations and frustrations as well as involving, from time to time, a financial burden.

Socialization: It should not take any sensitive person long to imagine the kind of social changes which take place as a person, once functioning with family, friends, work, and business associates in one gender role, shifts into another gender identity. A new life-style emerges. For many this may be a slow, evolving process; for others it may be quite dramatic. How will others react? What will the family do? How will a wife or husband respond? What changes will this new role bring in terms of an ongoing relationship to children? What about professional associates and business contacts? How about neighbors, fellow church members, and even close, long-time friends? One of the serious apprehensions lies in the question of who, in past and present, will stand by, will understand, will adjust as the process of change takes place, and what will be the final acceptance.

This role-change will surely bring about new friends, new relationships, new social groupings. There will be a different focus as to establishing close and intimate ties with others; there will be expectation and anticipation about physical and sexual contact, and there may very well be hopes and dreams about shared love and even marriage. Finding one's new role, new life, and new happiness may be a long process. Keith is just at the beginning. He will need all the help, all the understanding, all the love that family and friends can provide. Let us hope this will be his good fortune as "Kim" emerges and finds her place in life. Although the road is long and often tortuous for the transexual, there is the comfort of knowing that many have reached their goals and have found new joy, new satisfactions, and the peace which they should not be denied.

Postscript

Not long after the foregoing chapters were written and in final preparation for printing, an editorial appeared in the October 11, 1977 edition of *The Hartford Courant,* one of America's oldest newspapers. It is worthy that part of it be the basis of this postscript. The editor writes:

> Two civil liberties cases involving homosexual teachers came before the U. S. Supreme Court for review in its current term, but the justices declined to review them.
>
> Few issues before the court were more appropriate for consideration. The disappointing lack of review leaves other homosexuals open to continuing harassment, with legal protection subject to vague and conflicting state court rulings.
>
> Martin Luther wrote that "if all the world were composed of real Christians, that is, true believers, no prince, king, sword or law would be needed". . . .
>
> But such is not the case. Government often responds to the passions and prejudices and misguided zeal of certain elements of the population. The Supreme Court, with the Constitution as its guide, must protect unpopular minorities incapable of protecting themselves from the injustice.
>
> Homosexuals deserve protection from such vindictive behavior, inflicted at the whim of local communities. In more sophisticated cities, heterosexuality is not a job requirement. Such a basic right to privacy and freedom from governmental discrimination must be extended to homosexuals at the national level. . . .
>
> A beauty of the Constitution is its blindness to popularity.

The freedoms it extends don't designate approval, only protection from arbitrary behavior. Homosexuals, except in the most backwards of legal systems, are guilty of no crimes, responsible for no dangers to the Republic.

Although the adoption of new laws will surely bring comfort, relief, and protection to homosexuals, I do believe that we must recognize that the enforcement of legislation and court judgments are determined by human beings. These persons are often, if not usually, affected by the opinions and attitudes of the public. Therefore, it does become essential in the effort to provide social acceptance for those who comprise our sexual minorities, to try to reduce prejudice, misinformation, and lack of understanding as rapidly as possible. This has been one of the purposes of this book.

I trust it is clear that I have written as a Christian—one who believes that love is the central theme of the Gospel of our Lord Jesus Christ. As Norman Pittenger, Christian apologist and theologian, has stated so often in his lectures and his writing, "Man is born to be a lover." The letters heading the foregoing chapters are about persons eager to love; to love not only those to whom they are drawn but also to love those who comprise their families and their friends. They have asked for love in return.

At times it is not easy to love even though we ought to. Christians, others too, are well aware of Jesus' words "I command you that you love one another" (John 15:17). Intellectually this can be understood; emotionally it may provide disturbing challenge. Prejudice, preconceived ideas, and our own hidden agendas are not easily dispelled. However, when we recognize the changes of attitude that have taken place through the ecumenical movement, which has broken down many Christian denominational barriers; when we realize how many ethnic cultures have been woven into the fabric of American life; and when we see how many racial divisions have been bridged, then we have to have faith that little by little Bruce and Cindy, Gary and Keith, and the others of this book will find, along with the millions not unlike them, the love and the acceptance they would hope to receive.

Finally, it may have to be said that it is not always easy to extend our love and acceptance. To do so often means that we have to deal with changes within; we may even have to do an "about face" in order to respond to those who reach out to us. Although all of us know the need to be loved, I suspect we also recognize that it is being able to love which is even more important. The writer of the First Epistle of John speaks well to this:

> *There is no fear in love; but perfect love*
> *casteth out fear: because fear hath torment.*
> *He that feareth is not made perfect in love.*
> *We love him, because he first loved us.*
> *If a man say, I love God, and hateth his*
> *brother, he is a liar: for he that loveth*
> *not his brother whom he hath seen, how can*
> *he love God whom he hath not seen?*
>
> —1 John 4:18–20

Referral Resources

Parents of Gays, Metropolitan Duane Methodist Church, 201 West 13th Street, New York, New York 10011

Gay Parents Legal and Research Group, Box 1723, Lynnwood, Washington 98036

Lesbian Mothers National Defense Fund, 2446 Lorentz Pt., North Seattle, Washington 98109

Transvestites: Chevalier Publications, Box 36091, Los Angeles, California 90036

Transexuals: The Janus Information Facility, University of Texas, Medical Branch, Galveston, Texas 77550

Transvestites and Transexuals: Confide, Box 56 RH, Tappan, New York 10983

National Gay Task Force, 80 Fifth Ave., New York, New York 10011

For further and more detailed information about available counseling services in many centers and about gay organizations there are Guides and Directories of which a comprehensive one is Gay Yellowpages: The National Edition, Renaissance House, Box 292, Village Station, New York, New York 10014

Suggested Reading

Babuscio, Jack—*We Speak For Ourselves,* Camelot Press Ltd., South-
    ampton, England, 1976. Fortress Press, Philadelphia, 1977.
Bailey, Derrick Sherwin—*Homosexuality and the Western Christian Tradi-
    tion,* Longmans, Green and Co., London, 1955
Benjamin, Harry—*The Transsexual Phenomenon,* Julian Press, New
    York, 1966
Benson, R. O. D.—*In Defense of Homosexuality,* Julian Press, New York,
    1965
Brown, Howard—*Familiar Faces, Hidden Lives,* Harcourt Brace Jovano-
    vich, New York, 1976
Catholic Theological Society of America—*Human Sexuality,* Paulist
    Press, New York, 1977
Churchill, Wainwright—*Homosexual Behavior Among Males,* Hawthorn
    Books Inc., New York, 1967
Clark, Don—*Loving Someone Gay,* Celestial Arts, Millbrae, California,
    1977
Crew, Louie, Editor—*The Gay Academic,* ETC Publications, Palm
    Springs, California, 1977
Eglinton, J. Z.—*Greek Love,* Oliver Layton Press, New York, 1964
Feinbloom, Deborah Heller—*Transvestites and Transsexuals,* Delacorte
    Press, New York, 1976
Fisher, Peter—*The Gay Mystique,* Stein and Day, New York, 1972
Freedman, Mark—*Homosexuality and Psychological Functioning,* Brooks/-
    Cole, Monterey, California, 1971
Gearhart, Sally and Johnson, William—*Loving Women—Loving Men,*
    Glide Publ., San Francisco, 1974
Goergen, Donald—*The Sexual Celibate,* Seabury Press, New York, 1975
Gross, Alfred A.—*Strangers In Our Midst,* Public Affairs Press, Wash-
    ington, D.C., 1962

Hobson, Laura—*Consenting Adult,* Doubleday Inc., New York, 1975

Hoffman, Martin—*The Gay World,* Basic Books, New York, 1968

Horner, Tom—*Sex in the Bible,* Charles E. Tuttle Co., Rutland, Vermont, 1974

Isherwood, Christopher—*A Single Man,* Simon and Schuster, New York, 1964

———*Christopher and His Kind,* Farrar, Strans & Giroux, New York, 1976

Jones, Clinton R.—*Homosexuality and Counseling,* Fortress Press, Philadelphia, 1974

———*What About Homosexuality?* Thomas Nelson, Nashville, 1972

Jones, H. Kimball—*Toward a Christian Understanding of the Homosexual,* Association Press, New York, 1966

Katz, Jonathan—*Gay American History,* Thomas Crowell Co., New York, 1976

Kopay, David and Young, Perry—*The David Kopay Story,* Arbor House, New York, 1977

Mace, David R.—*The Christian Response to the Sexual Revolution,* Abingdon Press, Nashville, 1970

Marmor, Judd (editor)—*Sexual Inversion,* Basic Books, Inc., New York, 1965

Martin, Del and Lyon, Phyllis—*Lesbian/Woman,* Glide Publications, San Francisco, 1972

McNeill, John J.—*The Church and the Homosexual,* Sheed, Andrews and McMeel, Mission, Kansas, 1976

Miller, Merle—*On Being Different,* Random House, New York, 1971

Millett, Kate—*Sexual Politics,* Doubleday and Co., New York, 1970

Morris, Jan—*Conundrum,* Harcourt Brace Jovanovich, New York, 1974

Nicholson, Nigel—*Portrait of a Marriage,* Atheneum, New York, 1973

Oberholtzer, W. Dwight—*Is Gay Good?,* Westminster Press, Philadelphia, 1971

Pittenger, Norman—*Gay Lifestyles,* Universal Fellowship Press, Los Angeles, 1977

———*Making Sexuality Human,* Pilgrim Press, Philadelphia/Boston, 1970

———*Time for Consent,* S.C.M. Press Ltd., London, 1967

Prince, Virginia "Charles"—*The Transvestite and His Wife,* Argyle Books, Los Angeles, 1967

Reid, John—*The Best Little Boy in the World,* Putnam, New York, 1973

Renault, Mary—*The Last of the Wine,* Pantheon, New York, 1956

Silverstein, Charles—*A Family Matter,* McGraw-Hill, New York, 1977

Tripp, C. A.—*The Homosexual Matrix,* McGraw-Hill, New York, 1975

Valente, Michael F.—*Sex: The Radical View of a Catholic Theologian,* Bruce Publ. Co., New York, 1970

Warren, Patricia Nell—*The Front Runner,* William Morrow and Co., New York, 1974

———*The Fancy Dancer,* William Morrow and Co., New York, 1976

Weinberg, George—*Society and the Healthy Homosexual,* St. Martin's Press, New York, 1972

Weltge, Ralph W. (Editor)—*The Same Sex,* United Church Press, Philadelphia, 1969